SWU-NAP- 016

UNIFORMS OF RUSSIAN ARMY DURING THE NAPOLEONIC WAR VOL.11

UNDER THE REIGN OF ALEXANDER I
EMPEROR OF RUSSIA BETWEEN 1801 AND 1825
CAVALRY: HUSSARS, LANCERS, GENDARMES, & THE TRAIN

From the Viskovatov's greatest work:
"Historical description of the clothing and
arms of the Russian Army"

English translation by Mark Conrad

SOLDIERSHOP PUBLISHING

AUTHOR

Aleksandr Vasilevich Viskovatov born 22 April (4 May New Style) 1804, died 27 February (11 March) 1858 in St. Petersburg, Russian military historian. He graduated from the 1st Cadet Corps and served in the artillery, the hydrographic depot of the Naval Ministry, and then in the Department of Military Educational Institutions. He mainly studied historical artifacts and the histories of military units. Viskovatov's greatest work was the Historical Description of the Clothing and Arms of the Russian Army.

TRANSLATOR

Mark Conrad is an American historian with a great interest for all the Russian history.

PUBLISHING'S NOTE

NOTE ABOUT BOOK PRINTING BEFORE 1925

Title: **UNIFORMS OF RUSSIAN ARMY DURING THE NAPOLEONIC WAR VOL. 11**
C avalry: Hussars, Lancers, Gendarmes & the Train
By A.V.Viskovatov. English translation by Mark Conrad. First edition December 2016
Cover & Art Design: Luca S. Cristini. Plates re-colorations by Anna Cristini
ISBN code: 978-88-93271707

Published by Soldiershop publishing, via Padre Davide, 7 - 24050 Zanica (BG) ITALY. www.soldiershop.com

UNIFORMS OF THE RUSSIAN ARMY DURING THE NAPOLEONIC WAR VOL.11

UNDER THE REIGN OF ALEXANDER I EMPEROR OF RUSSIA BETWEEN 1801 AND 1825

*

Cavalry: Hussars, lancers, Gendarmes & the Train

Russian hussar at horse with lance by an engraving of Johann Cappi

HISTORICAL DESCRIPTION OF THE CLOTHING AND ARMS
OF THE RUSSIAN ARMY - A.V. VISKOVATOV
(First English translation by Mark Conrad)

Soldiershop is glad to presents the complete collection of the great job made by A.V. Viskovatov dedicated to the uniforms and weapons belonging to the Russian army during the Napoleonic period, until 1825. The time we considered corresponds to the reigns of two Tzars: Paul I, who reigned since 1769 until his murder on the 23rd of March 1801, and his son Aleksandr Pavlovi☐ Romanov, that with the title of Alexander I, sat on the throne until the 1st December 1825.

Our reprint in based on the original 19th century volumes, to be precise the volumes from 7 to 9 are dedicated to the reign of Paul I; this first part is distributed on 7 volumes, having a numbering from 1 to 7. From number 10 to 18 of the original volumes, the second part is dedicated to the Russian troops under Alexander I. These still being worked on and they will be soon ready, distributed on twenty volumes approximately. Our new edition, the first ever published in English, both on paper and digital format, boasts a large number of color plates, many of them unpublished and coloured by our team of expert artists and scholars of uniformology. Each volume is based on 50/70 plates, always accompanied by the original translated text which describes the uniforms, the organization and the armament of the Russian army of the period.

A unique work in its genre, a must have in any respecting collection!

Aleksandr Vasilevich Viskovatov born 22 April (4 May New Style) 1804, died 27 February (11 March) 1858 in St. Petersburg, Russian military historian. He graduated from the 1st Cadet Corps and served in the artillery, the hydrographic depot of the Naval Ministry, and then in the Department of Military Educational Institutions.

He mainly studied historical artifacts and the histories of military units. Viskovatov's greatest work was the Historical Description of the Clothing and Arms of the Russian Army (Vols. 1-30, St. Petersburg, 1841-62; 2nd ed. Vols. 1-34, St. Petersburg - Novosibirsk - Leningrad, 1899-1948). This work is based on a great quantity of archival documents and contains four thousand colored illustrations.

Viskovatov was the author of Chronicles of the Russian Army (Books 1-20, St. Petersburg, 1834-42) and Chronicles of the Russian Imperial Army (Parts 1-7, St. Petersburg, 1852). He collected valuable material on the history of the Russian navy which went into A Short Overview of Russian Naval Campaigns and General Voyages to the End of the XVII Century (St. Petersburg, 1864; 2nd edition Moscow, 1946). Together with A.I. Mikhailovskii-Danilevskii he helped prepare and create the Military Gallery in the Winter Palace.

He wrote the historical military inscriptions for the walls of the Hall of St. George in the Great Palace of the Kremlin. (From the article in the Soviet Military Encyclopedia.)

CONTENTS

*

Russian Army: Hussars, Lancers, Gendarmes, and the Train 1801-1825

CHANGES IN THE CLOTHING AND ARMAMENTS OF ARMY CAVALRY, FROM 1801 THROUGH 1825:

IV. Hussar Regiments
V.   Lancer Regiments
VI. Gendarme Regiment
VII. Army Train
Notes.

IV. HUSSAR REGIMENTS.

30 April 1802— Confirmation is given to a new table of **uniforms, accouterments,** and **weapons,** and on 25 May of this year colors are prescribed and rules laid down, on the basis of which Hussar regiments are to have:

Privates: pelisse [mentiya], dolman [dulaman], chakchiry pants, riding trousers [reituzy], boots [sapogi], neckcloth [galstuk], forage cap [furazhnaya shapka], smock [kitel], cloak [plashch], warm coat [fufaika], shako [kiver], saber with swordknot [sablya s temlyakom], swordbelt [portupeya], sabertache [tashka], sash [poyas], carbine [karabin], shoulder belt [pogonnaya perevyaz], cartridge pouch [lyadunka] with strap, and when mounted — a pair of *pistols [pistolety].* **Horse furniture and accessories** include: *saddle [sedlo] with holsters [olstredi], bridle [uzdechka], mouthpiece [mundshtuk], cruppers [pakhvi], chestband [papersti], saddle girth [podpruga], stirrups [stremena], cushion [podushka] for the pack load [vyuk], and small horse cloth [poponka]; saddlecloth [valtrap], valise [chemodan]. forage sack [furazhnyi sak], bag [torba], and water flask [vodonosnaya flyazha].*

Pelisse— of the regimental color, and the pattern is to be the same as in the previous reign, except with a high collar like that for all the preceding combat arms at this time; the pelisse is trimmed with white astrakhan fleece (Illus. 1491).

Dolman— of a particular color for each regiment; it is unchanged in pattern, like the pelisse, except for the collar (Illus. 1491).

Chakchiry pants— remain the same as before, of white cloth (Illus. 1491).

Riding trousers, as in Cuirassier and Dragoon regiments at this time, are of grey cloth, with covered buttons, and prescribed only for use on campaign (Illus. 1491).

Boots, with screwed-on spurs, have short, soft tops when worn with the riding trousers, and stiff tops reaching halfway up the calf when worn with chakchiry pants (Illus. 1491).

Forage cap— of the same color as the pelisse, with a band of the same color as the collar, or without any band at all, with a tassel and a ring around the top of the tassel; of the same pattern as for Cuirassiers and Dragoons.

Smock, of coarse calamanco, with covered buttons, prescribed to be of the same pattern as the smocks in Cuirassier and Dragoon regiments.

Cloak— made from grey cloth, with a similar grey standing collar with piping on its edges in the same colar as the dolman's collar, and with a flat button for fastening at the neck (Illus. 1492).

Warm coat, of sheepskin, as in all other regiments.

Shako, half-felt [*polupoyarkovyi*], black, 10 1/2 inches high. It has a flap which at its end has a black woollen tassel. It is trimmed along the upper and lower edges and along the edges of the flap with black woollen tape, from which is sewn on the right side a button loop that covers the socket for the plume and which has a cockade on its lower end with a flat button. This shako, to which are also attached two worsted cords with tassels (white in the 1st Battalion, and red in the 2nd), has a plume of white feathers and is held on by a thin strap of black leather (Illus. 1492 and 1493).

Saber, with a steel hilt, a scabbard with iron mountings, and swordknot. *Swordbelt* of red Russian leather, and *sabertache*, of the regimental color; these are the same as in the previous reign, except that the last has the monogram of EMPEROR ALEXANDER I.

Sash, of the same color as the pelisse, with slides [*perekhvaty*], a cord, and tassels of the same color as the braid on the pelisse and doloman. *Carbine*, with a red Russian leather firelock cover. Deerskin *shoulder belt*, whitened, with brass buckle, cross piece, and end piece, and iron hook. *Cartridge pouch* of red Russian leather, with the same kind of strap and with an iron ramrod [*priboinik*]. *Pistols*, with brass mountings. All *horse furniture* and the *saddlecloth* remain the same as they were under EMPEROR PAUL I, except the last item has a change in the monogram, while colors are in accordance with the description below.

In addition to these items, each Hussar squadron is issued 20 tinned copper *kettles* with covers, and 16 *sickles* for gathering hay.

Hussar horse— no higher than 5 feet tall, and no less than 4 feet 8 inches, of no particular prescribed colors, but authorized to cost 40 roubles not including delivery.

Noncommissioned officers and *first sergeants* [*vakhmistry*] have the same uniform as hussar privates, but with black astrakhan trim on the pelisse; with silver or gold galloon, according to the buttons, on pelisse and dolman collars and cuffs; cords and tassels on the shako are white with a mix of black of orange; white plumes with tops of mixed black and orange feathers, and chamois gloves without gauntlets, which are not at all authorized for privates (Illus. 1494 and 1495) (*). Like noncommissioned officers of the rest of the cavalry, hussar noncommissioned officers are authorized *stick canes*, and of the arms and accouterments of hussar privates, they do not have the carbine and its shoulder belt.

* Only in winter are hussar privates allowed to have cloth gloves, sewn from old uniforms.

Trumpeters [*trubachi*] are uniformed as hussar privates, with a red plume instead of white. They are also distinguished from privates by sewn-on chevrons [*nashivki*] or *rakoviny* ["shells"] of wool tape (in the same color as the braid) on the pelisse sleeves at the shoulder. They do not have: carbines, shoulder belts, or cartridge pouches, and in place of this last item each holster has six places or sockets for cartridges. Their keep their previous *trumpets* with wollen cords and tassels of the same color as the braid on the pelisse and dolman (Illus. 1496).

Staff-trumpeters [*shtab-trubachi*], with the same uniform and weapons as the preceding squadron trumpeters, are distinguished from them by the same features as noncommissioned officers have in comparison to Hussar privates (Illus. 1497). In addition, the cords and tassels on their trumpets are of three colors: white, black, and orange.

Officers of Hussar regiments, with the same colors and patterns of uniforms as Hussar privates, have grey Crimean lambskin [*merlushka*] trim on their pelisses; tracing [*tsifrovka*] or flat thin braid, galloon, and fringes (1 inch long), all gold or silver, in accordance with the particular assignments set forth below; shako with gold or silver (as on the pelisse and dolman) galloon trim and a thin fringe, with a similar small tassel at the end of the flap, with tassels and cords of silver with black and orange silk, and a plume of white feathers with black and orange at the base (Illus. 1498 and 1499). Sabers, swordknots, swordbelts, sabertaches, sashes, saddlecloths, and other horse furniture, except for the discontinued *sarsamy* [decorative leather harness — M.C.], remain of the same patterns as under EMPEROR PAUL I, and greatcoats are prescribed to be the same as for officers in the rest of the Army cavalry, with a standing collar in each regiment's own color, as set forth below. When in formation, and, in general, when carrying out duties, Hussar officers wear cartridge pouches over the left shoulder, similar to those described above for Dragoons and Horse-Jägers, with galloon and the other appointments.

When not on duty, Hussar officers are prescribed, in place of their previous *vengerki* [*"Hungarian"*, a kind of undress coat — M. C.], a dark-green cloth *undress coat [vitse-mundir]*, styled after the officers' coats used at this time in the infantry, but without horizontal pocket flaps. This has the usual hussar cuffs, tracing on the collar and cuffs in the color of the buttons, and red lining on the skirts and tails. With this undress coat are worn the standard cavalry hat and saber, with the swordbelt under the coat (Illus. 1500).

Noncombatant ranks of Hussar regiments are uniformed as noncombatants in Cuirassier and Dragoon regiments.

The *manner of wearing the **hair** and **queue*** in Hussar regiments is as under EMPEROR PAUL I, without any changes (157).

Colors for Hussar regiments' uniforms are prescribed as follows:

In the Mariupol Regiment, for lower ranks — blue [*sinii*] pelisse, white dolman, with yellow collar, cuffs, buttons, and braid; white sabertache with yellow trim; blue saddlecloths with yellow trim and braid (Illus. 1491, 1492, and 1493). For officers — gold trim and braid on the sabertache; white collar and cuffs on the undress coat, white collar on the greatcoat.

In the Pavlograd Regiment, for lower ranks — turquoise pelisse, dark-green dolman, with turquoise collar and cuffs, and yellow buttons and braid; dark-green sabertache with yellow trim; turquoise saddlecloths with yellow trim and dark-green braid (Illus. 1494). For officers — gold trim and braid on the sabertache; turquoise collar and cuffs on the undress coat, turquoise collar on the greatcoat (Illus. 1494).

In the Aleksandriya Regiment, for lower ranks — raspberry pelisse, dolman, collar, and cuffs, and white buttons and braid; raspberry sabertache with white trim; raspberry saddlecloths with white trim and braid (Illus. 1495). For officers — silver trim and braid on the sabertache; raspberry collar and cuffs on the undress coat, raspberry collar on the greatcoat.

In the Sumy Regiment, for lower ranks — turquoise pelisse, straw-colored [*palevyi*] dolman, with turquoise collar and cuffs, and white buttons and braid; turquoise sabertache with white trim; white saddlecloths with white trim and turquoise braid (Illus. 1496). For officers — silver trim and braid on the sabertache; turquoise collar and cuffs on the undress coat, turquoise collar on the greatcoat.

In the Akhtyrka Regiment, for lower ranks — brown pelisse and dolman, with yellow collar, cuffs, buttons, and braid; brown sabertache with yellow trim; brown saddlecloths with yellow trim and braid (Illus. 1497). For officers — gold trim and braid on the sabertache; brown collar and cuffs on the undress coat, brown collar on the greatcoat.

In the Yelisavetgrad Regiment, for lower ranks — straw-colored pelisse and dolman, with red collar and cuffs, yellow buttons and braid; red sabertache with straw-colored trim; red saddlecloths with straw-colored trim and braid (Illus. 1498). For officers — gold trim and braid on the sabertache; straw-colored collar and cuffs on the undress coat, straw-colored collar on the greatcoat.

In the Olviopol Regiment, for lower ranks — dark-green pelisse, dolman, collar, and cuffs, white buttons and braid; dark-green sabertache with white trim; dark-green saddlecloths with white trim and braid. For officers — silver trim and braid on the sabertache; dark-green collar and cuffs on the undress coat, dark-green collar on the greatcoat (Illus. 1499).

In the Izyum Regiment, for lower ranks — dark-blue [*temnosinii*] pelisse, red dolman; dark-blue collar and cuffs, yellow buttons and white braid; blue [*sinii*] sabertache with yellow trim; dark-blue saddlecloths with yellow trim and braid. For officers — gold trim and braid on the sabertache; blue collar and cuffs on the undress coat, blue collar on the greatcoat (Illus. 1500) (158).

14 June 1803 — The newly formed ***Belorussia* and *Odessa* Hussar Regiments** are prescribed: blue [*sinii*] pelisses; blue dolmans with red collars and cuffs; blue sabertaches and saddlecloths. Buttons and all trim: in the first regiment — white, in the second — yellow (Illus. 1501, 1502, and 1503). For combatant lower ranks, braid on the pelisse and dolman is ordered to be red with white, while shakos are cloth, with an attached visor, and two flaps for winter weather, as was established on 19 August, 1803, for noncombatant lower ranks in the Army infantry (Illus. 1502). *For hussar privates* these shakos have cords and tassels, or *kitish-vitish*, of red and white, with a red tassel or pompon and a white hair plume (Illus. 1501). *For trumpeters* — shakos have the same *kitish-vitish* and pompon as for privates, with a red plume (Illus. 1501). *For noncommissioned officers* — with the *kitish-vitish* in three colors: white, black, and orange; with a pompon divided into two white parts and two black and orange parts, and a white plume with a black top mixed with orange hair (Illus. 1502). *For staff-trumpeters* — with the same *kitish-vitish* and pompon as for noncommissioned officers and a red plume with a black and orange top (Illus. 1503). *Officers* of both regiments are given the same shakos, with white feather plumes with black and orange at the bottom; the *kitish-vitish* is silver with black and orange silk; silver pompon, while the sabertache and saddlecloth have monograms which—as all galloon, fringes, and tracery—are ordered to be silk: instead of silver — white, and instead of gold — yellow (Illus. 1503). The last replacement of silver and gold by silk is applied at this time in equal measure to officers' uniforms in the other Hussar regiments (159).

20 August 1803— These **shakos** described above are ordered to be introduced into all Hussar regiments, and beginning from this time, the former pattern of eagle on officers' sabertaches and saddlecloths is replaced by embroidered monograms and crowns, as in the Belorussia and Odessa Regiments (160).

8 October 1803— In the *Aleksandriya* Hussar Regiment the raspberry color for the pelisse, dolman, sabertache, and saddlecloth is changed to black (Illus. 1504) (161).

In 1804— The **hats** prescribed for wear by field and company-grade officers with their undress coats are ordered to be of the same pattern as those established at this time for field and company-grade officers of Cuirassier and Dragoon regiments, i.e. with a buttonhole loop of narrow galloon, of the same color as the buttons, and with a tall plume (162).

20 June 1806— For the newly formed *Grodno* **Hussar Regiment** there are prescribed: blue [*sinii*] pelisses and dolmans; sky-blue collars and cuffs; white buttons, red and white braid; blue sabertaches with a sky-blue toothed pattern and white braid and monogram (Illus. 1505) (163).

1 July 1806— There is the same change in uniforms of regimental and battalion **doctors** as described above in detail for Grenadier regiments (164).

1 October 1806— **Warm coats** [*fufaiki*] are withdrawn from lower ranks in Hussar regiments (165).

2 December 1806— Lower ranks lose their **queues** and **side curls** and are ordered to cut their hair short under a comb, while Generals and officers are allowed to proceed in this regard according to their own wishes (166).

12 March 1807— The newly established *Lubny* **Hussar Regiment** is ordered to have: blue [*sinii*] pelisses, dolmans, and chakchiry pants; this last item is trimmed with white worsted braid (the same color as the buttons); yellow collars and cuffs; white buttons; white and red braid; blue sabertaches with white trim; blue saddlecloths with yellow toothed trim; white braid and monograms on the saddlecloths (Illus. 1506). Around this time, the former **canes** for officers and noncommissioned officers are abolished (167).

20 November 1807— For all Hussar regiments, the **braid** on pelisses and dolmans is ordered to be of one color, as it was until the change of 1803 (168).

21 November 1807— In the Grodno Hussar Regiment, the white **chakchiry pants** are changed to blue with white trim, following the style of the chakchiry in the Lubny Regiment (169).

12 November 1808— When wearing the undress coat, Hussar officers are to wear dark-green **chakchiry** or **pants** (170).

4 February 1809— For all Hussar regiments, in order to spare Hussar officers the expense, uniforms with **gold** and **silver** (although discontinued in 1803, in time they again came into use) are ordered to be worn only on holidays and during reviews, and during the rest of the time they are to have worsted trim. Along with this, **pants** or **chakchiry** are introduced into all Hussar regiments, identical to those in the Lubny and Grodno regiments, except in the various colors described below in the entry for 11 November, 1809 (171).

11 February 1809— In place of their previous hats and forage caps with tassels, noncombatant lower ranks not holding noncommissioned officer rank are given new-pattern *caps[shapki]* identical with those which at this same time are introduced for Grenadier regiments, except that they are completely dark green with red piping around the edges of the band (172).

8 June 1809— The plumage on **generals' hats** (worn with the undress coat) is discontinued and the former style of buttonhole loop is replaced by a new one, made of four thick twisted cords of which the two middle ones are intertwined in braid-like fashion (173).

20 October 1809—Generals and field and company-grade officers of Hussar regiments are ordered to have *epaulettes* with the undress coat, following the pattern of epaulettes prescribed for these ranks in the rest of the Cavalry (Illus. 1507). In this same year, they are also given frock coats of dark-green cloth, with collars and cuffs in the same colors as on the dolman (174).

11 November 1809—All combatant ranks of Hussar regiments are to have *shakos[kivera]* of the same pattern as in use at this time in Grenadier regiments, with the plume, buttonhole loop, cockade, and button all as before, and with cords and a pompon in the same color as the braid on the dolman (Illus. 1508). Along with this change, and together with alterations in the way braid and galloon is sewn onto the pelisse, dolman, and chakchiry pants, as well as in the trim on sabertaches — the **colors** of uniforms, sabertaches, and saddlecloths in Hussar regiments are as follows:

In the Mariupol Regiment— blue [*sinii*] pelisse, dolman, and chakchiry; yellow collar and cuffs on the dolman; yellow braid, galloon, and buttons; blue sabertache and saddlecloth, with yellow trim and monograms (Illus. 1508).

In the Pavlograd Regiment— turquoise pelisse; dark-green dolman and chakchiry; turquoise collar and cuffs on the dolman; yellow braid, galloon, and buttons; dark—-reen sabertache and saddlecloth, with red trim and monograms (Illus. 1509).

In the Aleksandriya Regiment— black pelisse, dolman, and chakchiry; red collar and cuffs on the dolman; white braid, galloon, and buttons; black sabertache and saddlecloth, with red trim and monograms (Illus. 1509).

In the Sumy Regiment— grey pelisse and dolman; red chakchiry and collar and cuffs on the dolman; white braid, galloon, and buttons; red sabertache with white trim and monogram; grey saddlecloth, with red trim and monogram (Illus. 1509).

In the Akhtyrka Regiment— brown pelisse and dolman; blue chakchiry; yellow braid, galloon, and buttons; brown sabertache; blue saddlecloth; yellow trim and monograms on the sabertache and saddlecloth (Illus. 1510).

In the Yelisavetgrad Regiment— grey pelisse, dolman, and collar and cuffs on the dolman; dark-green chakchiry; yellow braid, galloon, and buttons; dark-green sabertache and saddlecloth, with yellow trim and monograms (Illus. 1510).

In the Olviopol Regiment— dark-green pelisse and dolman; red chakchiry and collar and cuffs on the dolman; white braid, galloon, and buttons (Illus. 1511); dark-green sabertache and saddlecloth, with red trim and monograms.

In the Izyum Regiment— blue pelisse; red dolman; blue chakchiry and collar and cuffs on the dolman; white braid, galloon, and buttons; red sabertache; blue saddlecloth; white trim and monograms on the sabertache and saddlecloth (Illus. 1512).

In the Belorussia Regiment— red pelisse; blue dolman and chakchiry; red collar and cuffs on the dolman; white braid, galloon, and buttons; red sabertache; blue saddlecloth; white trim and monograms on the sabertache and saddlecloth (Illus. 1512).

In the Grodno Regiment— blue pelisse, dolman, and chakchiry; sky-blue collar and cuffs on the dolman; white braid, galloon, and buttons; blue sabertache and saddlecloth, with sky-blue trim and monograms (Illus. 1513).

In the Lubny Regiment— blue pelisse, dolman, and chakchiry; yellow collar and cuffs on the dolman; white braid, galloon, and buttons; blue sabertache and saddlecloth, with white trim and monograms (Illus. 1513).

New-pattern **sabers** are given to all these regiments, whose scabbards remain as before, while the hilts have small arches [*duzhki*] (175).

16 June 1810— **Carbines** and **pistols** for Hussar regiments are ordered to be made according to the newly confirmed pattern. Both of these, and infantry muskets, are of identical caliber — seven lines, measured in English inches [i.e. 0.7 inches — M.C.] (176). In this same year the **plumes** on generals' and officers' hats are shortened (177).

23 September 1811— New-pattern *forage caps* are given to lower ranks of Hussar regiments, identical with those established at this time for Army infantry, Cuirassier, and Dragoon regiments, with the crown the same color as the dolman while the band is the same color as the collar and cuffs (178).

11 December 1811— In place of the uniform they have had since 1802, **noncombatant lower ranks** are given a new one identical to that established at this time for noncombatant lower ranks in Grenadier and Musketeer regiments (179).

In the beginning of 1812, all combatant ranks of Hussar regiments are given new **shakos**, identical with those authorized in this year for Horse-Jäger regiments, except with cords and a pompon in the same color as the braid on the uniform and with a buttonhole loop and scales in the same color as the buttons. Also, **collars** on the pelisse, dolman, cloak, and officer's undress coat are to be lower than before, without a slanted opening [*skos*] in front, and closed with small hooks (Illus. 1514) (180).

10 November 1812— **Carbines** and **bandoliers** are withdrawn from all Hussar regiments, and subsequently the only firearms left are pistols and sixteen musketoons [*mushketony*] in each squadron (181).

29 November 1812— In order to lessen their **expenses**, officers of Hussar regiments are allowed to have: instead of gold and silver appointments on their uniforms — white metal [*belevyi*] appointments, colored yellow or white; instead of silver shako cords, pompons, sashes and swordknots — white ones, of linen; and also linen galloon and embroidery on saddlecloths: instead of gold — orange, and instead of silver — white (182).

17 December 1812— The *Irkutsk* **Hussar Regiment**, renamed from Dragoons, is ordered to have: black pelisses, dolmans, sabertaches, and saddlecloths; raspberry chakchiry pants and collars and cuffs on dolmans; yellow buttons, braid, and galloon (Illus. 1515). Officers of this regiment receive pelisses and dolmans without fringes, with five rows of buttons (Illus. 1515), instead of as in other Hussar regiments where they have fringes and buttons in only three rows (183).

15 September 1813— Officers and combatant lower ranks of the *Akhtyrka, Belorussia, Aleksandriya,* and *Mariupol* Hussar regiments are awarded **badges for distinction** for the shako, of the same color as the buttons and in the form of a ribbon, with the Cyrillic inscription: *"za otlichie 14-go Avgusta 1813 goda"* [*"For distinction 14 August 1813"*] (Illus. 1516) (184).

6 April 1814— The **undress coats** of hussar officers are to be single-breasted with nine flat buttons; the collar is to be fastened with small hooks, and piping down the front is to be the same color as the collar. Dark-green pants are worn with these undress coats, and the same boots as in full dress, with small black tassels (Illus. 1517) (185).

3 May 1814— The *Sumy, Lubny,* and *Grodno* Hussar Regiments are awarded **badges for the shako**, like those received on 15 September, 1813, by the Akhtyrkha, Belorussia, Aleksandriya, and Mariupol regiments, with the inscription: *"Za otlichie"* (186).

20 May 1814— The grey **riding trousers** with buttons, used by hussar officers since 1802, are replaced by new ones: grey as before, with wide stripes and piping in the same color as the dolman's collar (Illus. 1518) (187).

19 August 1814— Similar **riding trousers**, except with leather on the seams, are given to lower ranks of Hussar regiments (Illus. 1518), and chakchiry pants are kept only for parades (188).

15 September 1814— Each Hussar regiment is given 1120 **carbines** and, in place of musketoons, 112 **rifles** [*shtutsera*] (Illus. 1519), which are to be worn on white bandoliers with brass buckles, cross pieces, and end pieces (189).

19 November 1814— The *Yelisavetgrad, Izyum,* and *Pavlograd* Hussar Regiments are awarded **badges for the shako**, like those received on 3 May, 1814, by the Sumy, Lubny, and Grodno Hussar Regiments. In this same year white tape is added to the **cockades** on officers' hats, this later being changed to silver (190).

16 April 1817— All Hussar regiments are ordered to have **shakos** with the plates confirmed at this time for Grenadier regiments. The regiments of the 3rd Hussar Division [should be "2nd"? C.f. Vol. 10 Part A – M.C.] — Akhtyrka, Aleksandriya, Mariupol, and Belorussia — keep their previous badges for excellence in the form of a ribbon, while the Sumy, Lubny, Grodno, Yelisavetgrad, Izyum, and Pavlograd regiments are given new ones in form of a shield, as in Army infantry regiments (191).

6 May 1817— **Trumpeters** of Hussar regiments are ordered to have wings [*kryltsy*] and chevrons on the sleeves of their pelisses and dolmans: the first item is to be the same color as the dolman collar, and the last — the same color as the braid (Illus. 1521) (192).

6 October 1817 — The **shakos** of officers and lower ranks in the Izyum Hussar Regiment are to have yellow scales, as well as shako plates and badges for distinction, to match the color of officers' buttons (Illus. 1522) (193), and in this same year *muskets[ruzhya]* are introduced into all Hussar regiments in place of carbines, of the same pattern as that confirmed at this time for Horse-Jägers, except without bayonets (194).

28 February 1819— Hussar regiments are ordered to carry new **sabers**, of the pattern used at this time by Horse-Jägers. In this same year, it is ordered that the **cartridge pouches** and **crossbelts** of red Russia leather used by noncommissioned officers and privates in these regiments are to be: the first item — of black, lacquered leather, with a round badge of yellow brass as in other Army cavalry regiments, a pistol ramrod on a white deerskin strap, and on a similar white deerskin crossbelt, which privates are to wear not over the right shoulder (as done up to this time), but over the left, under the bandolier (Illus. 1523) (195). After all these changes, in 1820 the **colors** for uniforms in Hussar regiments are as follows:

In the Sumy Regiment— grey pelisse; grey dolman; red collar and cuffs; red chakchiry; white braid, galloon, shako cords, pompon, and sash; red slides [*gomby*] on the sash; white buttons; red sabertache, with white trim and monogram; grey saddlecloth, with red trim and monogram and white braid (Illus. 1523).

In the Olviopol Regiment— dark-green pelisse and dolman; similarly colored collar and cuffs; red chakchiry; white braid, galloon, shako cords, pompon, and slides on the sash; red sash; white buttons; dark-green sabertache, with red trim and monogram; dark-green saddlecloth, with red trim and monogram and white braid (Illus. 1523).

In the Grodno Regiment— blue pelisse, dolman, and chakchiry; sky-blue collar and cuffs; white braid, galloon, shako cords, pompon, and slides on the sash; blue sash; white buttons; blue sabertache, with sky-blue trim and monogram; blue saddlecloth, with sky-blue trim and monogram and white braid (Illus. 1524).

In the Lubny Regiment— blue pelisse; blue dolman; yellow collar and cuffs; blue chakchiry; white braid, galloon, shako cords, pompon, and slides on the sash; blue sash; white buttons; blue sabertache, with white trim and monogram; blue saddlecloth, with white trim, monogram and braid (Illus. 1524.

In the Izyum Regiment— blue pelisse; red dolman; blue collar and cuffs; blue chakchiry; white braid, galloon, shako cords, pompon, and slides on the sash; blue sash; white buttons and shako chin scales for lower ranks, but yellow for officers (See the above entry for 6 October, 1817); red sabertache, with white trim and monogram; red saddlecloth, with white trim, monogram and braid (Illus. 1524.

In the Pavlograd Regiment— turquoise pelisse; dark-green dolman; sky-blue collar and cuffs; dark-green chakchiry; red braid, galloon, shako cords, pompon, and sash; turquoise slides on the sash; yellow buttons (Illus. 1525); dark-green sabertache, with red trim and monogram; dark-green saddlecloth, with red trim, monogram and braid.

In the Yelisavetgrad Regiment— grey pelisse, dolman, collar, and cuffs; dark-green chakchiry; red braid, galloon, shako cords, pompon, and sash; grey slides on the sash; yellow buttons; dark-green sabertache, with red trim and monogram (Illus. 1525); dark-green saddlecloth, with red trim, monogram and braid.

In the Irkutsk Regiment— black pelisse and dolman; raspberry collar, cuffs, and chakchiry; yellow braid, galloon, shako cords, pompon, and sash; black slides on the sash; yellow buttons (Illus. 1526); raspberry sabertache, with yellow trim and monogram; black saddlecloth, with raspberry trim and monogram and yellow braid.

In the Akhtyrka Regiment— brown pelisse and dolman; yellow collar and cuffs; dark-blue chakchiry; yellow braid, galloon, shako cords, pompon, and slide on the sash; sky-blue sash; yellow buttons; brown sabertache, with yellow trim and monogram; blue saddlecloth, with yellow trim, monogram, and braid (Illus. 1527).

In the Aleksandriya Regiment— black pelisse and dolman; red collar and cuffs; black chakchiry; white braid, galloon, shako cords, pompon, and sash; black slides on the sash; white buttons; black sabertache, with red trim and monogram; black saddlecloth, with red trim and monogram and white braid (Illus. 1527).

In the Mariupol Regiment— blue pelisse and dolman; yellow collar and cuffs; blue chakchiry; yellow braid, galloon, shako cords, pompon, and slides on the sash; blue sash; yellow buttons; blue sabertache, with yellow trim and monogram; blue saddlecloth, with yellow trim, monogram, and braid (Illus. 1528).

*In the Prince of Orange's Regiment (*The former *Belorussia Regiment.)*— red pelisse; blue dolman; red collar and cuffs; blue chakchiry; white braid, galloon, shako cords, pompon, and slides on the sash; red sash; white buttons; red sabertache, with white trim and monogram; red saddlecloth, with white trim, monogram, and braid (Illus. 1528) (196).

For Officers— braid, galloon, fringes, and monograms on the sabertache and saddlecloth are the same color as the buttons: gold or silver. Slides on the sash are silver, while the sash and shako cords are silver with black and orange silk (197).

16 February 1819— Hussar regiments are ordered to have ***covers*** for the shako and plume, identical to those established at this time for Dragoon and Horse—Jäger regiments (198).

20 February 1820— The shakos in Hussar regiments are ordered to have, instead of plumes, small oblong **plumes** or **pompons**: for lower ranks — of wool, the same color as the shako cords, and for officers — gold or silver, according to the color of the buttons (199).

18 April 1820— These **pompons** are abolished (200).

13 April 1821— Officers' **pelisses** and **dolmans** in Hussar regiments are to be without fringes, with five rows of buttons, following the example of the Irkutsk Hussar Regiment (Illus. 1529) (See the above entry for 17 December, 1812.) (201).

29 March 1825—For faultless service, **chevrons** sewn onto the left sleeve are established for combatant lower ranks: for 10 years of service — one; for 15 years — two; and for 20 — three, one over the other; all of yellow tape (202).

At the end of EMPEROR ALEXANDER I's reign, it is ordered that **horses** in Hussar regiments be assigned by the following colors:

In the first regiments of each division (Sumy, Izyum, and Akhtyrka) — sorrels.
In the second regiments (Olviopol, Pavlograd, and Aleksandriya) —blacks.
In the third regiments (Klyastitsy — renamed from the Grodno, Yelisavetgrad, and Mariupol) — grey.
In the fourth regiments (Lubny, Irkutsk, and Prince of Orange's) — chestnuts(203).

V. LANCER REGIMENTS.

In 1801, upon the ascension to the throne of EMPEROR ALEXANDER I, the *Tatar-Lithuanian [Tatarskii-Litovskii]* and *Polish Horse Regiments* receive new **uniforms** and **weapons** as follows:

a.) ***Tatar-Lithuanian Regiment***: rankers [sherengi] or *privates* — jacket [kurtka]; pants [pantalony]; girdle [kushak]; boots [sapogi]; neckcloth [galstuk]; headdress [shapka]; gloves [perchatki]; saber [sablya], with swordknot [temlyak]; swordbelt [portupeya]; cartridge pouch [lyadunka], with crossbelt [perevyaz], and, when in mounted order, *a pair of pistols [pistolety]*.

The ***jacket*** is blue [*sinii*], of cloth, with short skirts and tails; with lapels, pointed or slanted cuffs, with lining on the skirts and trim or piping along the edges of the collar, along the seams on the back, along the turnbacks, and along the sleeve seams, all of raspberry cloth; with two epaulettes of white worsted, and with tinned brass buttons (Illus. 1530).

Pants— of blue, with trim or stripes, and piping on the side seams, of raspberry cloth. These are long, to the heels; trimmed with black leather along the inner seam and fastened at the bottom with a small button, covered in raspberry cloth, and cords, likewise raspberry (Illus. 1530).

The ***belt***[*poyas*] [same item as the girdle [*kushak*] mentioned above — M.C.] is also of blue cloth, with two raspberry cloth stripes running down its length (Illus. 1530).

Bootsare round-toed, with short tops and with iron spurs screwed in above the heels.

Neckcloth, with dicky, of black cloth.

Shapkaheaddress— of raspberry cloth, with a black turn-up, like a cap band, trimmed along the edges with white worsted lace, with tassels and cords of white and raspberry worsted, and with a plume of white cock feathers (Illus. 1530).

Chamois ***gloves***, with short gauntlets.

Saber, ***swordknot***, and ***swordbelt*** — identical with those prescribed for hussars by the equipment table of 30 April, 1802.

Cartridge pouch— also of hussar pattern, except not of red Russian leather, but of black leather, worn on a whitened deerskin crossbelt, to which also belongs an iron hook for carrying the pistol (Illus. 1530).

Pistol— of the same pattern as for hussars, except with a brass ring on the butt, for attaching to the above-mentioned hook (Illus. 1530).

The ***saddle*** and all its accessories are prescribed to be as for hussars, while the ***saddlecloth*** is of dragoon style, of blue cloth with raspberry trim, with white braid along the edges, and with two IMPERIAL monograms and crowns of the same kind of braid (Illus. 1530).

Valise, of raspberry cloth; ***forage sack***, ***bag***, and ***water flask*** are all of the same patterns as for hussars.

Comrades[*tovarishchi*]are distinguished from rankers only in that in addition to the latter's prescribed weapons, they also have a lance [*pika*], with a red shaft and a pennon [*khoronzhevka* or *flyuger*] whose upper half is raspberry and lower half is blue. This lance's lower end is put in a small leather bucket [*bushmat*] fixed to the right stirrup, and at about its midpoint it has a strap of red Russian leather, similar to a swordknot, through which the man sitting on his horse passes his arm (Illus. 1530).

Noncommissioned officers, ***first sergeants*** [*vakhmistry*], ***deputies*** [*namestniki*] [Cadets? — M.C.], and also ***trumpeters***and ***staff-trumpeters***are distinguished from rankers and comrades in a manner similar to the way noncommissioned officers, trumpeters, and staff-trumpeters are distinguished from privates in in other regular cavalry regiments at this time.

Officers— wearing the same pattern and colors of uniform as privates or rankers, have silver buttons, epaulettes, galloon on the headdress and cartridge pouches, and braid on the saddlecloth, with a mix of black and orange silk. Plumes have a mixture of black and orange feathers at the base; the belt for the saber is black; black swordknot with silver stitching and tassel. When in formation, and in general while carrying out duties, they wear sashes [*sharfy*] identical to those used at this time by officers in other branches of the Russian Army (Illus. 1531).

*The manner of wearing the **hair** and **queue*** is the same as for other branches, except hussars, who wear side curls, as related above (204).

b.) ***Polish Horse Regiment*** — all combatant ranks differ from the same ranks of the preceding Tatar-Lithuanian Regiment only in that they have: blue [*sinii*] shapka headdresses; raspberry *collars*, with blue piping, and raspberry *saddlecloths* with blue trim. Also, the top halves of pennons in this regiment are blue, and the bottom halves are raspberry (Illus. 1532) (205).

For both regiments, there were no special instructions laid down regarding *noncombatants*.

29 March 1803— With the division of the Tatar-Lithuanian Regiment into two: the ***Tatar Horse Regiment*** and ***Lithuanian Horse Regiment***, the first is ordered to keep the previous uniform colors described above, while the second is to have white shapka headdresses with raspberry worsted tape (206).

30 March 1803— New tables are confirmed for uniforms and other items for the above mentioned two regiments, based on which they are given new-pattern **shapka headdresses**: higher than before, 9 1/2 inches; with a black leather band; with two peaks, of which the front one is put down while the back one is raised up, and with two chin straps fastening with a small leather button. The top and side edges, or curves, of the headdress are trimmed with white worsted tape, later changed to braid. On the left side of the headdress, above the socket in which is placed the plume, is sewn a white (the same color as the tape) worsted tassel, or pompon, and behind the small button fixed to the top of the crown, on the right side, is a doubled-over cord of white and blue worsted, with two tassels meeting this same description, and which is passed under the right epaulette and around the neck, and is fastened to the top botton of the left lapel, so that the tassels lie right against the left epaulette (Illus. 1533). This cord is called a *kitish-vitish*, which in time became *vitishkety*. *noncommissioned officers* have the headdress with the cord and pompon in three colors: white, black, and orange (Illus. 1533), while *officers' cords* are silver with black and orange silk. The pompon itself is silver with a monogram, as for officers of other branches. In the *Tatar Regiment* the headdress and covered button—at the right corner and serving to attach the cord—are raspberry, but white in the *Lithuanian Regiment* (Illus. 1533) (207). Along with this change in headdress, all ranks in both regiments are given: the same **riding trousers** used in other cavalry, of grey cloth, and also grey cloth **greatcoats**; blue **belts**, with a raspberry stripe down the middle; **cartridge pouches** and their **crossbelts**, completely identical to those for hussars, i.e. of red Russian leather, while **saddlecloths** do not have white braid along the edges of the trimming or lining (Illus. 1534). **Noncombatant ranks** are prescribed the exact same uniforms and weapons as authorized in other regiments of regular cavalry (208).

26 September 1803— ***THE TSAREVICH CONTANTINE PAVLOVICH'S Lancer Regiment***, renamed from the Odessa Hussar Regiment, is prescribed the following items of uniform, accouterments, and weaponry:

Lancer privates— blue *jacket*, of the pattern in use by the Tatar and Lithuanian Horse Regiments, but with the same skirts as on cuirassier kolet coats; with scarlet [*alyi*] collar, lapels, cuffs, piping, and lining on the skirts; with shoulder straps or epaulettes of yellow and red worsted; with yellow buttons, and also sewn-on bars on the collar and cuffs, of yellow tape [*bason*] with red tracery. *Pants* are blue with scarlet trim and piping and with black leather at the bottom. *Boots* have screwed-on iron spurs. The *belt* is blue with scarlet stripes and piping at the edges. The *headdress when in formation [stroevaya shapka]* is blue with worsted yellow and red braid, pompon, and cord. The *forage cap*, of the pattern used throughout the Army, is blue with a scarlet band, or without any band at all. *Riding trousers*, for campaign, are the same as in the rest of the cavalry. The *cloak* is as for hussars, of grey cloth, with a scarlet collar. *Gloves* (only for winter) are cloth, sewn from old uniforms. The *warm coat* is sheepskin. The *saber, swordknot, swordbelt,* and *carbine* are of the patterns for hussars. The *shoulder belt*, of leather from a dry cow [*yalovochnaya kozha*], is whitened; with a brass buckle, cross piece, and end piece, and an iron hook. The *cartridge pouch* is of black, lacquered leather, with the same plate as for cuirassiers and dragoons; with a small whitened strap for the pistol ramrod and with a crossbelt of similar material. *Pistols* are of the hussar pattern. The *saddlecloth* and all *horse furniture* is the same as in the Tatar, Lithuanian, and Polish Horse Regiments, except that the first item is blue with scarlet trim and likewise scarlet monograms and crowns, and edged with black braid, while the *valise* is grey (Illus. 1535).

Apart from these items, every Lancer squadron is issued with 20 brass *kettles* and 16 *sickles* for gathering hay.

Lancer horse— no taller than 5 feet, and not shorter than 4 feet 8 inches. There is no prescribed color, but the cost, less delivery fee, is authorized to be 40 roubles.

Carabinier-lancers [karabinery-ulany](16 in each squadron) have uniforms, accouterments, weapons, and all horse furniture as other lancers, except that the carbine is exchanged for the *rifle [shtutser]*, described above for the preceding regiments of Army cavalry. [Yes, this does say that carabinier-lancers differ from other lancers in that they *do not* have carbines – M.C.]

Noncommissioned officers and *first sergeants* of the Lancer regiment have the same uniform as lancer privates, but with gold galloon along the bottom and side edges of the collar and on the edges of the cuffs; they have the headdress's braid, pompon, and cords in white, orange, and black, and the top of the plume is black and orange feathers (Illus. 1536). Following the example of noncommissioned officers in the rest of the cavalry, they are authorized *stick canes*, and of the weapons carried by lancer privates, they do not have the carbine, and the cartridge pouch is not worn over the right shoulder, as privates do, but over the left.

Distinguished officer candidates [portupei-yunkera], having the same uniform, weapons, and horse furniture as the other noncommissioned officers described above, also have officers' swordknots.

Trumpeters, also uniformed as lancer privates, with a red plume instead of white, are further distinguished from them by sewn-on trim, of yellow woollen lace: on the back's side seams, down and across the sleeves, along the skirts and tails, collar, and shoulder wings. Of lancer weapons, they do not have the carbine and cartridge pouch, in place of which each of their holsters has six places or sockets for cartridges, while their *trumpets* are the same as for hussars, with cords and tassels of yellow and red worsted (Illus. 1537).

A *staff-trumpeter* is distinguished from the preceding squadron trumpeters in that, similar to noncommissioned officers, he has his jacket's collar and cuffs with gold galloon;, a plume with a top of black and orange feathers; white, mixed with black and orange, cords and tassels for the trumpet, and a stick cane (Illus. 1537) (209).

Officers of the Lancer regiment, wearing uniforms of the same colors and pattern as for lancer privates, have (on the collar and cuffs) lace-bars embroidered in gold; gold epaulettes; silver braid and headdress cords, with black and orange silk; silver pompon; white plume with black and orange feathers at the base; gold galloon along the bottom edge of the headdress, along the straps of the swordbelt, and on the cartridge pouch's crossbelt, in the last case with two silver plates and two prickers of the same material, on small chains; swordknots and sashes are the same as in the rest of the cavalry, while saddlecloths have gold galloon along the edges of the red trim and likewise gold embroidered monograms (Illus. 1538) (210).

Noncombatants, both lower ranks and officers, are prescribed the same uniform and weapons as noncombatants in the rest of the cavalry (211).

20 March 1805— The *Polish Horse Regiment* is given new uniforms, following the pattern used in the Tatar and Lithuanian regiments, except with a blue headdress, with its braid and cords of white and blue worsted (Illus. 1539) (212).

26 February 1806— THE TSAREVICH CONSTANTINE PAVLOVICH'S **Lancer Regiment** is ordered to have **greatcoats** instead of cloaks, with a scarlet collar, tabs under it, and shoulder straps (213).

2 May 1806— In the same regiment, carbines are replaced by *lances*, with black shafts and the same taffeta pennons as in the Tatar, Lithuanian, and Polish regiments, with the top half scarlet, and the bottom half white. As a consequence of this, the shoulder belt is taken away (except for Lancer-Carabiniers, who have rifles), and the cartridge pouches begin to be worn on the right side (Illus. 1540) (214).

1 October 1806— **Warm coats** are withdrawn from lower ranks in the Lancer and Horse regiments (215).

2 December 1806— Lower ranks of the Tatar, Lithuanian, Polish, and THE TSAREVICH'S Lancer regiments are ordered to cut off their **queues**, leaving their hair cut short under a comb. In this regard, however, generals and field and company-grade officers are allowed to proceed according to their own wishes (216).

29 April 1807— The newly established *Horse-Volhynia* **Regiment** is prescribed all the same uniform items, accouterments, and weapons as THE TSESAREVICH'S Lancer Regiment, except with raspberry instead of scarlet, with white lace sewn on the coats of trumpeters instead of yellow, and without lace-bars on the collar and cuffs (217).

17 September 1807— Generals and field and company-grade officers of the above four Horse and Lancer regiments are ordered to have new pattern *epaulettes*, following the model confirmed at this time for Generals and officers of other cavalry, and for lower ranks these are issued with a thick fringe that does not hang down (218). In this same year, **canes** are discontinued for officers and noncommissioned officers (219).

11 November 1807—The *Polish, Tatar,* and *Lithuanian Lancer Regiments*, renamed from Horse regiments, are ordered to conform to THE TSESAREVICH'S Lancer Regiment in regard to all **accouterments** and **weapons**, as well as the pattern of **tails on the jacket**. The same applies to the Volhynia Regiment, in existence since 29 April, and which also receives the title of Lancers (220).

5 August 1808— The following **uniform colors** are confirmed for Lancer regiments.

For *HIS HIGHNESS THE TSAREVICH'S Lancers* — red collar, lapels, and cuffs; yellow buttons, blue headdress; red trim on pants and saddlecloth; red pennons in the 1st Battalion; in the 2nd — red upper half to the pennon, with a narrow white stripe, and a white lower half, with a narrow red stripe (Illus. 1541).

For the *Polish Lancers* — raspberry collar, lapels, and cuffs; white buttons, blue headdress; raspberry trim on pants and shabrack; blue pennons in the 1st Battalion; in the 2nd — blue upper half to the pennon, with a narrow raspberry stripe, and a raspberry lower half, with a narrow blue stripe (Illus. 1542).

For the *Tatar Lancers* — blue collar with raspberry piping; raspberry lapels and cuffs; white buttons, raspberry headdress; raspberry trim; raspberry pennons in the 1st Battalion; in the 2nd — raspberry upper half to the pennon, with a narrow white stripe, and a white lower half, with a narrow raspberry stripe (Illus. 1543).

For the *Lithuania Lancers* — blue collar with raspberry piping; raspberry lapels and cuffs; white buttons, white headdress; raspberry trim on pants and shabrack; white pennons in the 1st Battalion; in the 2nd — white upper half to the pennon, with a narrow blue stripe, and a blue lower half, with a narrow white stripe (Illus. 1544).

For the *Volhynia Lancers* — blue collar with raspberry piping; raspberry lapels and cuffs; yellow buttons, blue headdress; raspberry trim on pants and shabrack; in the 1st Battalion — yellow top half to the pennon, with a narrow white stripe, and a white lower half, with a narrow yellow stripe; in the 2nd — yellow upper half to the pennon, with a narrow raspberry stripe, and a raspberry lower half, with a narrow yellow stripe (Illus. 1545).

Jackets, pants, belts, and saddlecloths in all five regiments are left blue, as before, while the grey **greatcoats** have tabs and shoulder straps the same color as the jacket collar. Beginning at this time, the tops of lower ranks' **shapka headdresses** are lined with black leather for strength, and the feather plumes are replaced by **hair plumes**, of the same style as used at this time by hussars. Officers' headdresses are ordered to have only one chinstrap, with metal fittings (the same color as the buttons), in the form of a small chain (Illus. 1546), while noncommissioned officers and privates, including trumpeters, are to have two straps, with fittings of the very same color, but in the form of scales (Illus. 1546) (221).

18 August 1808— The *Chuguev Lancer* Regiment, renamed from a Cossack regiment, is ordered to have all its uniforms and weaponry patterned after those in THE TSAREVICH'S Lancer Regiment, except with white appointments instead of yellow; with red headdresses instead of blue; with white lace sewn onto trumpeters' coats, instead of yellow, and without sewn-on tabs or lace-bars on the collar and cuffs. Pennons: red in the 1st Battalion, and in the 2nd — red upper half with a narrow blue stripe, and blue lower half with a narrow red stripe (Illus. 1547) (222).

11 February 1809— In place of their previous hats and forage caps with tassels, **noncombatant lower ranks** not holding noncommissioned officer rank are given new-pattern *caps*, identical with those which at this same time are introduced for Cuirassier, Dragoon, and Hussar regiments (223).

4 April 1809— **Noncommissioned officers** are ordered to have galloon sewn not on the bottom and side edges of the collar, but on the top and side edges (224).

20 November 1811— Instead of being taffeta, **pennons** on the lances of all Lancer regiments are to be of nankeen [*kitaichatyi*], without any change in colors (225).

11 December 1811— In place of the uniform they have had since 1802, **noncombatant lower ranks** are given a new one identical to that established at this time for noncombatant lower ranks in Cuirassier, Dragoon, and Hussar regiments (226).

29 November 1812— In order to lessen their **expenses**, officers of Lancer regiments are allowed to have: instead of gold and silver fittings on their epaulettes—bronze, colored yellow or white; instead of silver sashes and swordknots—white ones, of linen: and also linen monograms on saddlecloths: instead of gold—orange, and instead of silver—white. Also, swordbelts and cartridge pouches are ordered to be whitened, without galloon (227).

In this same year, the **collars** of jackets and greatcoats in all Lancer regiments are ordered to be lower than before, and closed with small hooks. Thin **plumes** are issued, wider at the top than at the bottom, while **sabers** are to be in all-iron scabbards, with an iron lattice, or arches, on the hilt. In addition, the leather lining on **pants** is taken away (Illus. 1548) (228).

17 December 1812— The **Lancer regiments renamed from Dragoons** are prescribed blue jackets, pants, girdles, and saddlecloths, with the following distinctions:

For the *Yamburg* — raspberry collar, lapels, cuffs, piping, wide stripes on the pants, stripes on the girdle, and trim on the saddlecloth; yellow buttons, epaulettes, and headdress cords; white shapka headdress, with red braid and pompon; white top half to the pennon, with a narrow raspberry stripe, and a raspberry lower half, with a narrow white stripe (Illus. 1548).

For the *Orenburg* — raspberry collar, lapels, cuffs, piping, wide stripes on the pants, stripes on the girdle, and trim on the saddlecloth; yellow buttons, epaulettes, and headdress cords; raspberry shapka headdress, with yellow braid and pompon; blue top half to the pennon, with a narrow raspberry stripe, and a raspberry lower half, with a narrow blue stripe (Illus. 1548).

For the *Zhitomir* — red collar, lapels, cuffs, piping, wide stripes on the pants, stripes on the girdle, and trim on the saddlecloth; white buttons, epaulettes, and headdress cords; blue shapka headdress, with white braid and pompon; yellow top half to the pennon, with a narrow blue stripe, and a blue lower half, with a narrow yellow stripe (Illus. 1549).

For the *Siberia* — red collar, lapels, cuffs, piping, wide stripes on the pants, stripes on the girdle, and trim on the saddlecloth; white buttons, epaulettes, and headdress cords; white shapka headdress, with red braid and pompon; yellow top half to the pennon, with a narrow white stripe, and a white lower half, with a narrow yellow stripe (Illus. 1550).

For the *Vladimir* — blue collar; red lapels, cuffs, piping, wide stripes on the pants, stripes on the girdle, and trim on the saddlecloth; yellow buttons, epaulettes, and headdress cords; blue shapka headdress, with yellow braid and pompon; yellow top half to the pennon towards the shaft, but blue towards the end, with a narrow blue stripe, and a lower half with the colors reversed and with a yellow stripe (Illus. 1551).

For the *Taganrog* — blue collar; red lapels, cuffs, piping, wide stripes on the pants, stripes on the girdle, and trim on the saddlecloth; yellow buttons, epaulettes, and headdress cords; white shapka headdress, with red braid and pompon; yellow top half to the pennon towards the shaft, but red towards the end, with a narrow red stripe, and a lower half with the colors reversed and with a yellow stripe (Illus. 1552).

For the *Serpukhov* — blue collar; red lapels, cuffs, piping, wide stripes on the pants, stripes on the girdle, and trim on the saddlecloth; yellow buttons, epaulettes, and headdress cords; red shapka headdress, with yellow braid and pompon; blue top half to the pennon towards the shaft, but red towards the end, with a narrow red stripe, and a lower half with the colors reversed and with a blue stripe (Illus. 1553) (229).

In all these regiments, *privates* have white hair plumes, and monograms and crowns on the saddlecloth in the same color as its trim. For *noncommissioned officers*, the collar and cuffs on the jacket have galloon of the same color as the buttons; the top of the plume is black with orange. For *trumpeters*, sewn-on lace is white and plumes are red. *Officers'* uniform distinctions, as well as all the accouterments and weapons of the above seven regiments, are the same as in the four old regiments: Polish, Tatar, Lithuania, and Volhynia. (230).

(Note: On 12 December, 1809, THE TSAREVICH'S Lancer Regiment had joined the Guards.)

20 May 1814— The campaign **riding trousers** with buttons, used by Lancer officers since 1803, are replaced by new ones: grey as before, with two wide stripes and piping, of the same color as the wide stripes and piping on the blue pants, and without leather on the inner seams (Illus. 1554) (231).

25 July 1814— Lancer regiments are ordered to remake their *coats* in the style confirmed for Lancer regiments in the Polish forces, i.e. with almost the same kind of tails as were in the Tatar, Lithuanian, and Polish Horse Regiments from 1801 to 1808 (Illus. 1554) (232).

19 August 1814— Lower ranks of Lancer regiments are given new-pattern *riding trousers*, similar to those established on 20 May for officers, except with leather at the foot (Illus. 1554) (233).

11 December 1815— Officers of Lancer regiments are given *rock coats*, of a pattern identical to that established for officers of other regular forces, but in blue, with a similar blue lining, and collar, cuffs, and buttons of the same colors as on the dress coat (Illus. 1555) (234).

28 February 1817— **Officers** of Lancer regiments are ordered to have galloon on the swordbelt straps and cartridge-pouch crossbelts in the same color as the buttons — gold or silver; plates on the crossbelts, prickers, and small chains are always silver; headdress cords are also silver, with a mix of black and orange only within the tassels (235).

6 May 1817— It is confirmed that in all Lancer regiments, whatever the button color may be, the trim on **trumpeters' jackets** is to be white tape, and wings are to be the same color as the lapels and cuffs (236).

8 October 1817— The *Bug Lancer Regiments*, renamed from Cossack regiments, are prescribed the same uniform clothing as other lancers. Buttons are to be white for all, while distinctive colors are as follows:

For the 1st Bug Lancer Regiment— light-blue collar, lapels, cuffs, piping, wide strips on the pants, stripes on the girdle, and trim on the saddlecloth; light-blue shapka headdress, with red braid and pompon; sky-blue top half to the pennon, with a narrow white stripe, and a white lower half, with a narrow sky-blue stripe (Illus. 1556).

For the 2nd Bug Lancer Regiment— yellow collar, lapels, cuffs, piping, wide strips on the pants, stripes on the girdle, and trim on the saddlecloth; yellow shapka headdress, with white braid and pompon; yellow top half to the pennon, with a narrow white stripe, and a white lower half, with a narrow yellow stripe (Illus. 1557).

For the 3rd Bug Lancer Regiment— white collar, lapels, cuffs, piping, wide strips on the pants, stripes on the girdle, and trim on the saddlecloth; white shapka headdress, with red braid and pompon; white pennon (Illus. 1558).

For the 4th Bug Lancer Regiment— light-green collar, lapels, cuffs, piping, wide strips on the pants, stripes on the girdle, and trim on the saddlecloth; light-green shapka headdress, with yellow braid and pompon; light-green top half to the pennon, with a narrow white stripe, and a white lower half, with a narrow light-green stripe (Illus. 1559) (237).

12 April 1818— All Lancer regiments are told to not wear **plumes** until further orders (238).

26 June 1818— The Lancer regiments making up the *Lithuania Lancer Division* — *Polish, Tatar, Lithuania*, and *Volhynia* — are ordered to have, with their previous blue uniform, raspberry collars, lapels, cuffs, piping, wide stripes on the pants, stripes on the girdles, and trim on saddlecloths; white buttons, epaulettes, and headdress cords. Shapka headdresses and pennons are by regiments: in the *Polish* Regiment — blue (Illus. 1560), in the *Tatar* — raspberry (Illus. 1561), in the *Lithuania* — white (Illus. 1562), in *Volhynia* — light blue (Illus. 1563). Along with this, these headdresses are ordered to be of a new pattern: with only one front peak; with raised convex scales, with white lace on the curves of the crown and around the band; with a white bottom pompon, a white oblong pompon or small plume, and a white plate in front, of the same shape as used at this time on the shakos of dragoons, horse-jägers, and hussars (Illus. 1564) (239).

Along with this, the four regiments of the *Ukraine Lancer* Division, renamed from Cossacks, are prescribed the following distinctive colors with their blue uniform and yellow buttons:

For the 1st Ukraine Lancer Regiment — raspberry collar, lapels, cuffs, piping, stripes on the girdle, wide stripes on the pants, and trim on the saddlecloth; yellow shapka headdress, with red braid; yellow top half to the pennon, with a narrow white stripe, and a white lower half, with a narrow yellow stripe (Illus. 1565).

For the 2nd Ukraine Lancer Regiment — red collar, lapels, cuffs, piping, stripes on the girdle, wide stripes on the pants, and trim on the saddlecloth; green shapka headdress, with red braid; green top half to the pennon, with a narrow white stripe, and a white lower half, with a narrow green stripe (Illus. 1566).

For the 3rd Ukraine Lancer Regiment — light-blue collar, lapels, cuffs, piping, stripes on the girdle, wide stripes on the pants, and trim on the saddlecloth; light-blue shapka headdress, with red braid; light-blue top half to the pennon, with a narrow white stripe, and a white lower half, with a narrow light—blue stripe (Illus. 1567).

For the *4th Ukraine Lancer Regiment* — white collar, lapels, cuffs, piping, stripes on the girdle, wide stripes on the pants, and trim on the saddlecloth; white shapka headdress, with red braid; white pennon (Illus. 1568) (240).

16 February 1819— For Lancer regiments, when on campaign, *covers* are established for headdresses and plumes, of raven's duck or Flemish linen, painted with black oil paint, in the manner of oilskin, so that they do not allow water to pass through them. Detailed directives in this regard include the following:

1.) The cover is to be sewn following the headdress, i.e. four-cornered and with a peak, and so that it can be more easily put on and taken off, its sides, from the left to the right, must not be stitched tight, but fastened with small hooks, and have a small indentation in back.

2) This cover must cover the bottom pompon, and so at this point it has a socket which is lined with cloth of the same color as the pompon, and instead of the pompon the headdress is to have a small piece of wood, similar to the discussion above about shako covers for dragoons.

3) On the front of the cover, in the center (meaning between the top and bottom), are to be sewn, made of yellow cloth: the squadron N<u>o</u>— on the right side of the headdress, 1/2 inch from the front edge, and the Cyrillic letter E [for *eskadron*] — on the left, at the same distance (Illus. 1569).

4) A piece of oilskin, painted on both sides, is sewn onto the bottom edge of the cover. Its width fits the two back sides of the headdress, and it is 7 inches long. Its purpose is the same as described above in the description of the cover for dragoon shakos.

5) The cover, number, and letter are to be cleaned in the same way as related above for covers for dragoons (241).

At this same time it was directed that during winter, all combatant Lancer regiments are to have their **lapels** closed and fastened with buttons, while in summer, as well as in parades and on holidays, these are to be open, and held by small hooks (242).

4 April 1819— Lower ranks of Lancer regiments are to have blue **pants** with sewn-on leggings [*kragi*] of black leather, as they had previously up to 1812 (Illus. 1570) (243).

21 and 24 July 1819— In all Lancer regiments, **shapka headdresses** are ordered to all be of one pattern — that confirmed in the preceding year for regiments of the Lithuania Lancer Division, and in all regiments the buttons, epaulettes, lace on the headdress, and all metal appointments are to be of one color: white. Uniforms and saddlecloths are left blue, and the following colors are established to distinguish regiments:

a.) 1st Lancer Division:
Vladimir Regiment— red shapka headdress; red top half to the pennon, with a narrow white stripe, and a white lower half, with a red stripe (Illus. 1570).

Siberia Regiment— white shapka headdress; blue top half to the pennon, with a narrow white stripe, and a white lower half, with a blue stripe (Illus. 1571).

Orenburg Regiment— yellow shapka headdress; yellow top half to the pennon, with a narrow white stripe, and a white lower half, with a yellow stripe (Illus. 1572).

Yamburg Regiment— light-blue shapka headdress; light-blue top half to the pennon, with a narrow white stripe, and a white lower half, with a light-blue stripe (Illus. 1573).

In all four of these regiments, the collar, lapels, cuffs, piping, wide stripes on the pants, stripes on the girdle, and trim on the saddlecloth are all red.— In the regiments of the 1st and 2nd Lancer Divisions: *Vladimir, Siberia, Orenburg, Yamburg, Taganrog, Chuguev, Borisoglebsk,* and *Serpukhov*, the bands on **forage caps** are ordered to be the same color as the regulation shapka headdresses (246). In this same year, **trumpeters' jackets** in Lancer regiments are ordered to be trimmed with white lace, somewhat modified, and more thickly on the sleeves than before. (Illus. 1584) (247).

20 March 1825 — [Sic, should be 29 March - M.C.] Sewn-on **chevrons** on the left sleeve are established for combatant lower ranks who have rendered faultless service: for 10 years service—one, for 15 years—two, and for 20 years—three, one above the other; all of yellow tape (248).

VI. GENDARME REGIMENT.

10 June 1815— The officers and lower ranks chosen from all Cavalry regiments to be Gendarmes [*Zhandarmy*] are directed to have a **red arm band** [*perevyazka*] on the right are to distinguish themselves from others (249).

30 August 1815— The personnel of the *Gendarme* (renamed from the Borisoglebsk Dragoons) *Regiment*, are ordered to have the following **uniform clothing** and **weapons**:

Privates— single-breasted coat, of light-blue cloth; with a similar colored collar, cuffs, and infantry-pattern cuff-flaps; with red cloth shoulder straps and piping; with white worsted aiguilettes on the left shoulder; with white buttons (in one row down the front) and with light-blue lining. *Pants;* worn with *high boots; short boots* for riding trousers, and *riding trousers* identical to those which the regiment had before being renamed from Dragoons, except with red trim, or wide stripes, and piping. *Gloves* do not have gauntlets. The *greatcoat*, of the previous pattern, but in light-blue, has red collar piping, cuff-flaps, and shoulder straps, and white buttons. The *forage cap* is light blue, with the same color band, and red piping on the top and around both edges of the band. The *helmet, swordbelt, broadsword, swordknot, musketoon* or*musket* (with a bayonet, sling, and firelock cover), *cartridge pouch, crossbelt* (for the cartridge pouch and, at the same time, the musketoon) with *hook, pistols*, and all *horse furniture*, are all as for dragoons, except that the color of the *saddlecloth*, which is prescribed to be light blue with the same color trim, or lining, around it, while piping, monograms, and crowns are of red cloth. The *valise* is grey (Illus. 1585).

Noncommissioned officers— ordered to have the same items as privates, except the musketoon. The coat has silver galloon on the collar and cuffs (Illus. 1586); the swordknot tassel is white, with black and white; the cartridge-pouch crossbelt is narrow and the saddle has no saddle bucket.

Trumpeters— prescribed all the same items as privates, with the exception of the musketoon, cartridge pouch, and saddlebucket. The *coat* has light-blue wings and white sewn-on lace; the *helmet* has red plumage; *trumpets* are brass, with white tassels and cords (Illus. 1587).

Staff-trumpeters— as distinct from the preceding squadron trumpeters, they are prescribed the same distinctions as authorized for noncommissioned officers as compared to privates, while trumpet cords and tassels are white, with black and orange (Illus. 1587) (250).

Officers— keep their previous dragoon uniform, only with a change in colors, which for them are to be the same as for lower ranks, and with the addition of silver embroidered lace-bars on the collar and cuff-flaps of the coat. For them, epaulettes, aiguilette, and the saddlecloth's monogram with crown are silver (in accordance with the color of the buttons) (Illus. 1588, 1589, and 1590) (251).

15 May 1817— All ranks in the Gendarme Regiment, when in formation or on parade, are ordered to have **gloves** with gauntlets, as for cuirassiers. **Cuffs** on the coat are to be slit, without flaps, following the pattern for cuirassiers and dragoons (with two silver lace-bars for officers), and the scales on the **helmets** are raised and convex. For lower ranks, shoulder straps are replaced by worsted **epaulettes** with fringes; privates are also given **bandoliers** for their muskets, and **pistol ramrods** are directed to be on the cartridge pouches, following the example of lancers and hussars (Illus. 1591 and 1592) (252).

8 July 1820— In the same regiment, all combatant ranks are ordered to have white trim on the **saddlecloths** instead of light-blue (Illus. 1593), while **trumpeters' sewn-on lace** on coats is to be closer together than before, and not straight across the wings, but at a slant to the bottom edge (Illus. 1593) (253).

29 March 1825— Sewn-on **chevrons** on the left sleeve are established for combatant lower ranks who have rendered faultless service: for 10 years service — one, for 15 years — two, and for 20 years — three, one above the other; all of yellow lace (254).

VII. ARMY TRAIN.

9 May 1819— Confirmation by HIGHEST AUTHORITY is given to the following **uniform clothing** and **weapons** for the *Train battalions* established for the first four Army Corps:

*For **privates** and **master craftsmen** [masterovye]* — single-breasted coat, of dark-grey, with light-blue collar, slit cuffs, piping on the skirts and tails, and shoulder straps, with grey lining and white buttons (in one row down the front). *Riding trousers* are dark grey, with light-blue wide stripes and piping. *Boots* have no spurs. The *shako* is the infantry model, but without cords; with chin scales of white tin, or with scales and with a single chin strap (according to the decision of immediate commanders); with a ribbon or cockade of black tape edged in orange; with a black buttonhole loop and a light-blue pompon. Chamois *Gloves*, without gauntlets. The *greatcoat* cloth is grey, or of white mixed with grey hairs; with a light-blue collar and shoulder straps and white buttons. *Forage caps* are grey, with a light-blue band and the company number, in yellow braid, on the band. The *saber and swordbelt* are of the current patterns for the horse-artillery and horse-jägers. The *swordknot* is of red Russian leather, with a woollen tassel, colored according to company, as in infantry battalions (Illus. 1594). *Water flask* of the infantry pattern. The *knapsack [ranets]* (for master craftsmen) is also the infantry model, and the *valise* is as for the cavalry. The latter item is of grey cloth.

Noncommissioned officers— are ordered to be distinguished by silver galloon on the collar and cuffs of the coat, and by the shako pompon and swordknot tassel appropriate to this rank. All their horse furniture is to be lancer style, except for the color of the saddlecloth, which for them is prescribed to be dark grey like the coat, with light-blue trim and piping. Monograms and crowns are also light-blue, but trimmed with black braid (Illus. 1595).

Officers— the *coat* is to be the same as for privates in regard to cut and color, with with skirts and tails as for infantry officers, and with silver epaulettes. *Riding trousers, boots,* and *gloves*—of the same patterns as for lower ranks. The *shako* is as for lower ranks, but with scales for all officers, and silver cords, pompon, and buttonhole loop. It also has white tape around the cockade. *Hat* — of the standard officers' pattern, with a white plume. *Saber*—of the horse-artillery and horse-jäger pattern, and for those officers with one inscribed *"Za khrabost" ["For courage"]*— with a gold hilt. *Swordbelt*—all of the pattern for the horse-artillery or horse-jägers, with stitched-on silver galloon. *Swordknot* — of the pattern for officers throughout the cavalry. *Sash*—of the pattern for officers throughout the Army. *Saddlecloth, valise,*and all *horse furniture* in general—following lancer patterns; colors are as related above for noncommissioned officers, except the monograms and crowns are embroidered silver (Illus. 1596) (255).

25 October 1819— Lower ranks of Train battalions are ordered to have corps **numbers** on their shoulder straps, cut out right through and backed by sewn-on yellow cloth, and around the straps is cloth piping: in the *1st Battalion* — red; *in the 2nd* — white, *in the 4th* — green, and *in the 3rd* — without piping (Illus. 1594 and 1595) (256). These same colors are also adopted for piping around the top edges of the **forage caps** (257).

6 June 1820— The cockade on **shakos** in Train battalions is replaced by a single-flame grenade, of white tin (Illus. 1597) (258).

27 September 1820— The following newly established Train brigades are ordered to have **letters and numbers** (yellow on light-blue shoulder straps):

a)*For the brigade with the Grenadier Corps* — the Cyrillic letter *G.*
b) *For the brigade with the 2nd and 3rd Reserve Cavalry Corps* —*№1* and the Cyrillic letter *K.*
c)*For the brigade with the 4th and 5th Reserve Cavalry Corps* — *№ 2* and the Cyrillic letter *K.*
d)*For the brigade with the Separate Lithuania Corps* — the Cyrillic letter *L,* and in addition, this last brigade has raspberry piping on the collar and cuffs (Illus. 1598).

The distinctions for the battalions in each brigade remain the same as established on 25 October, 1819 (259).

6 January 1821— Train battalions of the *Grenadier Corps* are ordered to have on their **shakos**, instead of a grenade

— a white tin plate, of the pattern in use by the Grenadier and Carabinier regiments of this corps (Illus. 1599) (260).

15 March 1822— Field and company-grade officers of the Train are given grey *frock coats* with light-blue collars, similar cuffs, white buttons, and grey linings (Illus. 1600) (261).

5 January 1823— The *1st Battalion of the Lithuania Train Brigade*, of which one half is with the Guards troops in Warsaw, and the other half with the Grenadier Brigade of the Separate Lithuania Brigade, is ordered to have **shakos** with grenadier-pattern plates (Illus. 1601) (262).

20 April 1823— Lower ranks of this brigade are ordered to have **shakos** with round blue woollen pompons, while officers are to have round silver ones (Illus. 1602) (263).

29 March 1825— Sewn-on **chevrons** are established for faultless service by combatant lower ranks, based on the same rules and of the same pattern as described above for Army Cavalry regiments (264).

Russian hulans by an engraving of Johann Cappi

APPENDIX: Notes to the Illustrations

By Mark Conrad.

1514. Research by A. Valkovich (*"Armeiskie Gusary 1812-1816: Novye Materialy"*, in *Tseikhgauz* No. 1 - 1991) modifies what Viskovatov has provided.

Firstly, the majority of hussar regiments received lances in April-May of 1812. Three regiments—the Belorussia and Oliviopol, with the Danube Army, and the Lubny, in the Crimea—were apparently armed with lances later. Only the first rank carried the lance—640 authorized for each regiment, or 64 for each squadron. Experience in training with the lance soon revealed that the carbine on the bandolier interfered with its handling, so the front ranks' carbines were sent to replacement squadrons. The order was also given that for hussars armed with lances, pelisses were either to be left with the wagon train or worn with arms in the sleeves; they were not to be worn loose like a cape. The lances were usually of the pattern for lancers, but with black shafts and no pennons. However, the Pavlograd and Izyum regiments appear to have ignored this, and had turquoise-white and red-blue pennons, respectively (Elberfeld manuscript - February, 1814). And once in October, 1812, the Akhtyrka Regiment put pennons on their lances to deceive the enemy into thinking they were Polish cavalry. These lances were also carried by hussar regiments during the 1815 march back to France.

Viskovatov also missed certain details of hussar uniforms. Research shows that the Yelisavetgrad and Pavlograd regiments adopted red braid, shako cords, and pompons some time before the 1812 campaign.

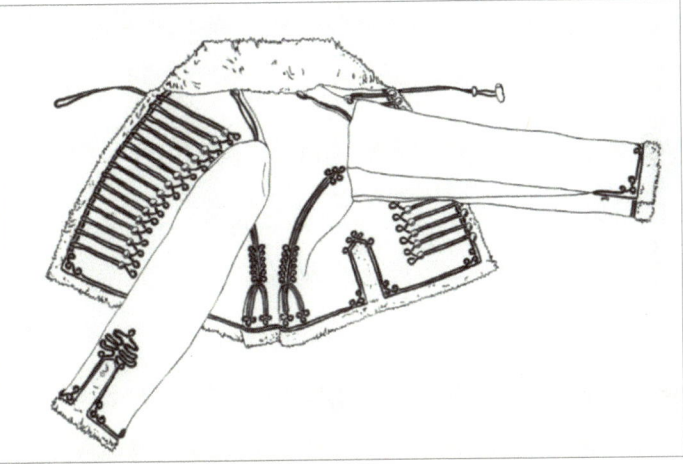

▲ *Private's pelisse, Pavlograd Hussar Regiment, 1809-1812. From Valkovich's depiction of an actual item in the Russian State Historical Museum.*

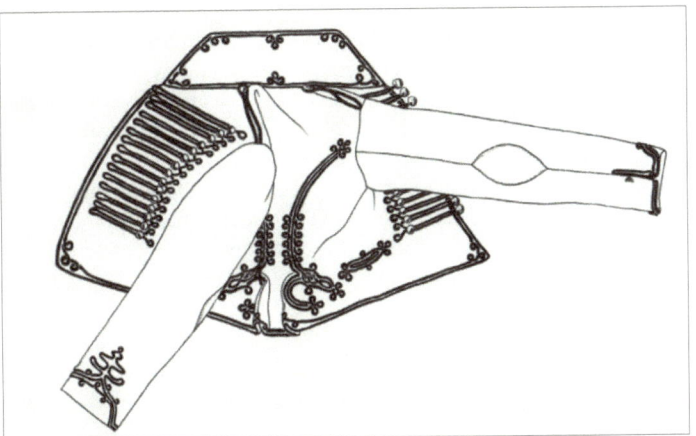

▲ *Private's doman, Pavlograd Hussar Regiment, 1809-1812. From Valkovich's depiction of an actual item in the Russian State Historical Museum.*

Furthermore, Viskovatov records that hussar privates were to have white fleece trim on their pelisses. However, new research shows that the difficulty in keeping this clean led to some regiments using black at least as early as 1808. An official description of hussar uniform distinctions in 1816, but most probably valid for the 1812 campaign, shows the Sumy, Belorussia, Mariupol, Yelisavetgrad, and Irkutsk regiments using black fleece for their lower ranks. A general order directing all regiments to change to black fleece was only issued in November, 1826.

The same 1816 source also shows that cloaks and officers' greatcoats had collars in the facing colors, most likely this having been the case since the changes in hussar uniforms in 1809-1811.

NOTES

(157) Everything stated here about clothing, weapons, and horse furniture for combatant and noncombatant ranks in Hussar regiments is based on: HIGHEST confirmed table of 30 April, 1802; descriptions in PSZ, Vol. XLIV, pg. 55, № 20,279, and pg. 29, № 20,109; information received from the Commissariat Department of the War Ministry; the drawings mentioned above in Note 71, and evidence from contemporaries.

(158) Ibid.

(159) PSZ, Vol. XL, pg. 188, № 30,309. information received from the Commissariat Department of the War Ministry; drawings in the SOVEREIGN EMPEROR'S Own Library, catalog № 361; actual items preserved in various Arsenals and at the Commissariat Department of the War Ministry, and evidence from contemporaries.

(160) Announcement from the Military College to the Military Commission, 20 August, 1803; information from the Commissariat Department of the War Ministry, and .

(161) PSZ, Vol. XLIV, pg. 56, № 20,972.

(162) Evidence from contemporaries.

(163) PSZ, Vol. XLIV, pg. 56, № 22,185.

(164) Ibid., pg. 31, № 22,197.

(165) Information from the Commissariat Department of the War Ministry.

(166) HIGHEST Directive announced to the Military College by the Minister of Military Land Forces, 2 December, 1806.

(167) PSZ, Vol. XLIV, pg. 56, № 22,491.

(168) Ibid., № 22,692.

(169) Ibid., № 22,693.

(170) Information from the Commissariat Department of the War Ministry.

(171) PSZ, Vol. XLIV, pg. 57, № 23,470.

(172) Ibid., Vol. XXX. pg. 781, № 23,478.

(173) Ibid., pg. 1006, № 23,695.

(174) Ibid., pg. 1219, № 23,919.

(175) Ibid., Vol. XLIV, pg. 57, № 23,470; information received from the Artillery and Commissariat Departments of the War Ministry; actual items of Hussar uniforms and weaponry from that time, preserved in HIS IMPERIAL HIGHNESS THE GRAND DUKE MICHAEL PAVLOVICH'S Own Arsenal and at the Commissariat Department, and evidence from contemporaries.

(176) PSZ, Vol. XXXI, pg. 215, № 24,263.

(177) Evidence from contemporaries.

(178) Information received from the Commissariat Department of the War Ministry.

(179) PSZ, Vol. XLIV, pg. 31 №№ 24,911 and 24,912, and evidence from contemporaries.

(180) Information received from the Commissariat Department of the War Ministry; evidence from contemporaries, and contemporary portraits and drawings.

(181) PSZ, Vol. XXXII, pg. 454, № 25,262.

(182) Ibid., Vol. XLIV, pg. 57, № 25,278.

(183) Ibid., pg. 57, № 25,292; see the text in the entry for 13 April, 1821.

(184) HIGHEST Order and information received from the Commissariat Department of the War Ministry.

(185) PSZ, Vol. XLIV, pg. 133, № 25,565.

(186) HIGHEST Order and information received from the Commissariat Department of the War Ministry.

(187) Information received from the Commissariat Department of the War Ministry, and evidence from conteporaries.

(188) Ibid.

(189) Information received from the Commissariat Department of the War Ministry; evidence from conteporaries, and contemporary drawings, including those mentioned above in Note 120.

(190) HIGHEST Order; information received from the Commissariat Department of the War Ministry, and evidence from contemporaries.

(191) PSZ, Vol. XLIV, pg. 138, № 26,801.

(192) Information received from the Commissariat Department of the War Ministry, and contemporary drawings.

(193) PSZ, Vol. XLIV, pg. 134, № 27,079.

(194) *Description of the Tula Arms Factory*, cited in Note 150.

(195) Information received from the Commissariat and Artillery Departments of the War Ministry.

(196) Information received from the Commissariat Department of the War Ministry, where models of hussar uniform items from that time are preserved, and evidence from contemporaries.

(197) Ibid.

(198) PSZ, Vol. XLIV, pg. 101, № 27,681.

(199) Ibid., pg. 134, № 28,153.

(200) Order of the Chief of HIS IMPERIAL MAJESTY'S Main Staff, 18 April, 1820, №21.

(201) The kind of order, from 13 April, 1821, № 11.

(202) PSZ, Vol. XL, pg. 188, № 30,309.

(203) Evidence from contemporaries.

(204) Information about the uniforms and weapons of these two regiments—the Tatar-Lithuanian and Polish—is taken from contemporary documentation on items of their uniform clothing, accouterments, and weaponry. Also used as sources were drawings preserved in the SOVEREIGN EMPEROR'S Own Library, catalog №246, sheets 35 and 36.

(205) Ibid.

(206) PSZ, Vol. XXVII, № 20,694, pg. 521.

(207) Ibid., Vol. XLIII, Part II, continuation of the first section, pg. 17, № 20,695; HIGHEST confirmed table of uniform, accouterment, and weaponry items of the Tatar and Lithuanian Horse Regiments, 30 March, 1803; actual shapka headdresses preserved in the SOVEREIGN EMPEROR'S Own Arsenal; information received from the Commissariat Department of the War Ministry, and evidence from contemporaries.

(208) The same volume of PSZ and the same table mentioned in the preceding note.

(209) HIGHEST confirmed table of uniform, accouterment, and weaponry items for a Lancer regiment, 26 September 1803: actual articles preserved in Arsenals and at the Commissariat Department of the War Ministry; information received from this Department, and evidence of contemporaries.

(210) Ibid.

(211) Ibid.

(212) HIGHEST confirmed table of uniform, accouterment, and weaponry items for the Polish Horse Regiment, 20 March 1805.

(213) Proposal of the Intendant-General of the Army to the Commissariat Office, 26 February 1806, and information received from the Commissariat Department of the War Ministry.

(214) Proposal of the Intendant-General of the Army to the Commissariat Office, 2 May, 1806, and information received from the Commissariat Department of the War Ministry.

(215) Information received from the same Department.

(216) PSZ, Vol. XXIX, pg. 901, № 22,382.

(217) PSZ, Vol. XXIX, № 22,526, pg. 1184, and information received from the Commissariat Department of the War Ministry.

(218) Information received from the Commissariat Department of the War Ministry.

(219) Ibid.

(220) Ibid.

(221) PSZ, Vol. XLIV, Part II, Fourth Sect., in *Ukases Regarding Uniforms*, pg. 57, № 23,205; actual items kept in Arsenals and by the Commissariat Department of the War Ministry; information received from this Department, and evidence from contemporaries.

(222) PSZ, Vol. XXX, № 23,232, pg. 530, and information received from the Commissariat Department of the War Ministry.

(223) PSZ, Vol. XXX, pg. 781, № 23,478, and information received from the Commissariat Department of the War Ministry.

(224) Information received from the Commissariat Department of the War Ministry.

(225) PSZ, Vol. XLIV, pg. 57, № 24,883.

(226) Ibid., pg. 31, №№ 24,911 and 24,912, and evidence from contemporaries.

(227) Ibid., pg. 50, № 25,278, and information received from the Commissariat Department of the War Ministry.

(228) Information received from this Department; actual items from this time, preserved at this Department and various Arsenals; contemporary portraits and drawings, and evidence from contemporaries.

(229) PSZ, Vol. XLIV, pg. 58, № 25,242, and information received from the Commissariat Department of the War Ministry.

(230) Information received from this same Department.

(231) Ibid.

(232) PSZ, Vol. XLIV, pg. 102, № 26,018, and information received from the Commissariat Department of the War Ministry.

(233) Information received from this same Department, and the same volume of PSZ, pg. 120, № 25,644.

(234) PSZ, Vol. XLIV, pg. 102, № 26,018, and pg. 135, № 26,019.

(235) Information received from the Commissariat Department of the War Ministry.

(236) Ibid.

(237) Information received from this same source, and PSZ, Vol. XXXIV, pg. 794, №27,081.

(238) Information received from the Commissariat Department of the War Ministry.

(239) Information received from this same Department, and PSZ, Vol. XLIV, pg. 137, № 27,392.

(240) Information received from the Commissariat Department of the War Ministry.

(241) PSZ, Vol. XLIV, pg. 101, № 27,260.

(242) Evidence from contemporaries.

(243) Information received from the Commissariat Department of the War Ministry.

(244) PSZ, Vol. XLIV, pg. 135, № 27,899; pg. 136, №№ 27,900 and 28,183, and model items preserved in the Commissariat Department of the War Ministry.

(245) PSZ, Vol. XLIV, pg. 136, № 27, 984.

(246) Ibid., № 28,355, a) .

(247) Model uniforms from this year, kept at the Commissariat Department of the War Ministry, and information received from this Department.

(248) PSZ, Vol. XL, pg. 188, № 30,309.

(249) Order to the Army, by the Commander-in-Chief, General-Field Marshal Barclay de Tolly, 10 June 1815.

(250) Information received from the Commissariat Department of the War Ministry.

(251) Ibid.

(252) Information received from the same source; Order of the Chief of HIS IMPERIAL MAJESTY'S Main Staff, 15 May,1817, № 45, and engravings by Maj. Gen. Kiel, mentioned above in Note 120.

(253) Information received from the same Department, and the model items themselves, preserved here.

(254) PSZ, Vol. XL, pg. 188, № 30,309.

(255) Model uniform clothing, preserved at the Commissariat Department of the War Ministry, and the Archive of the Inspection Department of this same Ministry, in the file regarding the formation of Train battalions for the Independent Lithuania Corps, 1820, № 430, sheet 107.

(256) PSZ, Vol. XLIV, pg. 139, № 27,955.

(257) Information received from the Commissariat Department of the War Ministry, and the file cited above in Note 255.

(258) Information received from this same Department.

(259) PSZ, Vol. XLIV, pg. 139, № 28,429.

(260) Order of the Chief of HIS IMPERIAL MAJESTY'S Main Staff, 6 January, 1821, №1.

(261) PSZ, Vol. XLIV, pg. 139, № 28,969.

(262) Ibid., pg. 137, № 29,256.

(263) Ibid., № 30,325, and information received from the Commissariat Department of the War Ministry.

(264) Ibid., Vol. XL, pg. 188, № 30,309.

РИСУНКИ
ОДЕЖДЫ и ВООРУЖЕНІЯ
РОССІЙСКИХЪ
ВОЙСКЪ
1801-1825.

PLATES LIST OF ILLUSTRATIONS

1546. Officer's and Soldier's Shapka Headdresses. Tatar Lancer Regiment. 1808-1811.

1547. Privates. Chuguev Lancer Regiment. 1808-1811.

1548. Company-grade Officer of the Yamburg Lancer Regiment. NCO of the Orenburg Lancer Regiment. 1812-1814.

1549. Trumpeter. Izyum Lancer Regiment. 1812-1814.

1550. Private and Staff-Trumpeter. Siberia Lancer Regiment. 1812-1814.

1551. Company-grade Officer. Vladimir Lancer Regiment. 1812-1814.

1552. Field-grade Officer and Private. Taganrog Lancer Regiment. 1812-1814.

1553. Private. Serpukhov Lancer Regiment. 1812-1814.

1554. Company-grade Officer and Private. Serpukhov Lancer Regiment. 1814-1818.

1555. Company-grade Officers. Serpukhov Lancer Regiment. 1815-1818.

1556. Private. 1st Bug Lancer Regiment. 1817 and 1818.

1557. Private and Noncommissioned Officer. 2nd Bug Lancer Regiment. 1817 and 1818.

1558. Trumpeter. 3rd Bug Lancer Regiment. 1817 and 1818.

1559. Private and Company-grade Officer. 4th Bug Lancer Regiment. 1817 and 1818.

1560. Private. Polish Lancer Regiment. 1818 and 1819.

1561. Noncommissioned Officer. Tatar Lancer Regiment. 1818 and 1819.

1562. Trumpeter. Lithuania Lancer Regiment. 1818 and 1819.

1563. Field-grade Officer. Volhynia Lancer Regiment. 1818 and 1819.

1564. Soldier's and Officer's Shapka Headdresses. Volhynia Lancer Regiment. 1818 and 1819.

1565. Private and Officer. 1st Ukraine Lancer Regiment. 1818 and 1819.

1566. Noncommissioned Officer. 2nd Ukraine Lancer Regiment. 1818 and 1819.

1567. Trumpeter and Private. 3rd Ukraine Lancer Regiment. 1818 and 1819.

1568. Field-grade Officer. 4th Ukraine Lancer Regiment. 1818 and 1819.

1569. Noncommissioned Officer. 4th Ukraine Lancer Regiment. 1819.

1570. Field-grade Officer and Private. Vladimir Lancer Regiment. 1819-1825.

1571. Noncommissioned Officer. Siberia Lancer Regiment. 1819-1825.

1572. Trumpeter. Orenburg Lancer Regiment. 1819-1820.

1573. Company-grade Officer. Yamburg Lancer Regiment. 1819-1825.

1574. Privates. Taganrog and Chuguev Lancer Regiments. 1819-1825.

1575. Staff-Trumpeters. Borisoglebsk and Taganrog Lancer Regiments. 1819-1825.

1576. Private. 1st Ukraine Lancer Regiment. 1819-1825.

1577. Noncommissioned Officers. 2nd, 3rd, and 4th Ukraine Lancer Regiments. 1819-1825.

1578. Noncommissioned Officers. 1st and 2nd Bug Lancer Regiments. 1819-1825.

1579. Company-grade Officers. 3rd and 4th Bug Lancer Regiments. 1819-1825.

1580. Privates. Polish Lancer Regiment. 1819-1825.

1581. Noncommissioned Officer. Tatar Lancer Regiment. 1819-1825.

1582. Trumpeter. Lithuania Lancer Regiment. 1819-1825.

1583. Field-grade Officer and Company-grade Officer. Volhynia Lancer Regiment. 1819-1825.

1584. Trumpeters. Volhynia Lancer Regiment. 1820-1825.

1585. Privates. Gendarme Regiment. 1815-1817.

1586. Noncommissioned Officer. Gendarme Regiment. 1815-1817.

1587. Trumpeter and Staff-Trumpeter. Gendarme Regiment. 1815-1817.

1588. Company-grade Officer. Gendarme Regiment. 1815-1817.

1589. Field-grade Officers. Gendarme Regiment. 1815-1817.

1590. Field-grade Officers. Gendarme Regiment. 1815-1825.

1591. Noncommissioned Officer and Company-grade Officer. Gendarme Regiment. 1817-1825.

1592. Private. Gendarme Regiment. 1817-1820.

1593. Noncommissioned Officer and Trumpeter. Gendarme Regiment. 1820-1825.

1594. Privates. Train Battalions. 1819 and 1820.

1595. Noncommissioned Officers. Train Battalions. 1819 and 1820.

1596. Company-grade Officers. Train Battalions. 1819 and 1820.

1597. Noncommissioned Officer and Company-grade Officer. Train Battalions. 1820-1825.

1598. Noncommissioned Officer. Lithuania Train Brigade. 1820-1825.

1599. Company-grade Officer. Train Battalions of the Grenadier Corps. 1821-1825.

1600. Company-grade Officer. Lithuania Train Brigade. 1822-1825.

1601. Noncommissioned Officer. 1st Battalion of the Lithuania Train Brigade. 1823-1825.

1602. Private and Company-grade Officer. 1st Battalion of the Lithuania Train Brigade. 1823-1825.

Private. Mariupol Hussar Regiment. 1802-1803.

Private. Mariupol Hussar Regiment. 1802-1803.

Hussar Shako. 1802-1803.

Noncommissioned Officer. Pavlograd Hussar Regiment. 1802-1803.

Noncommissioned Officer. Aleksandriya Hussar Regiment. 1802-1803.

Trumpeter. Sumy Hussar Regiment. 1802-1803.

Staff-Trumpeter. Akhtyrka Hussar Regiment. 1802-1803.

Officer. Yelisavetgrad Hussar Regiment 1802-1803.

Officer. Olviopol Hussar Regiment. 1802-1803.

1500

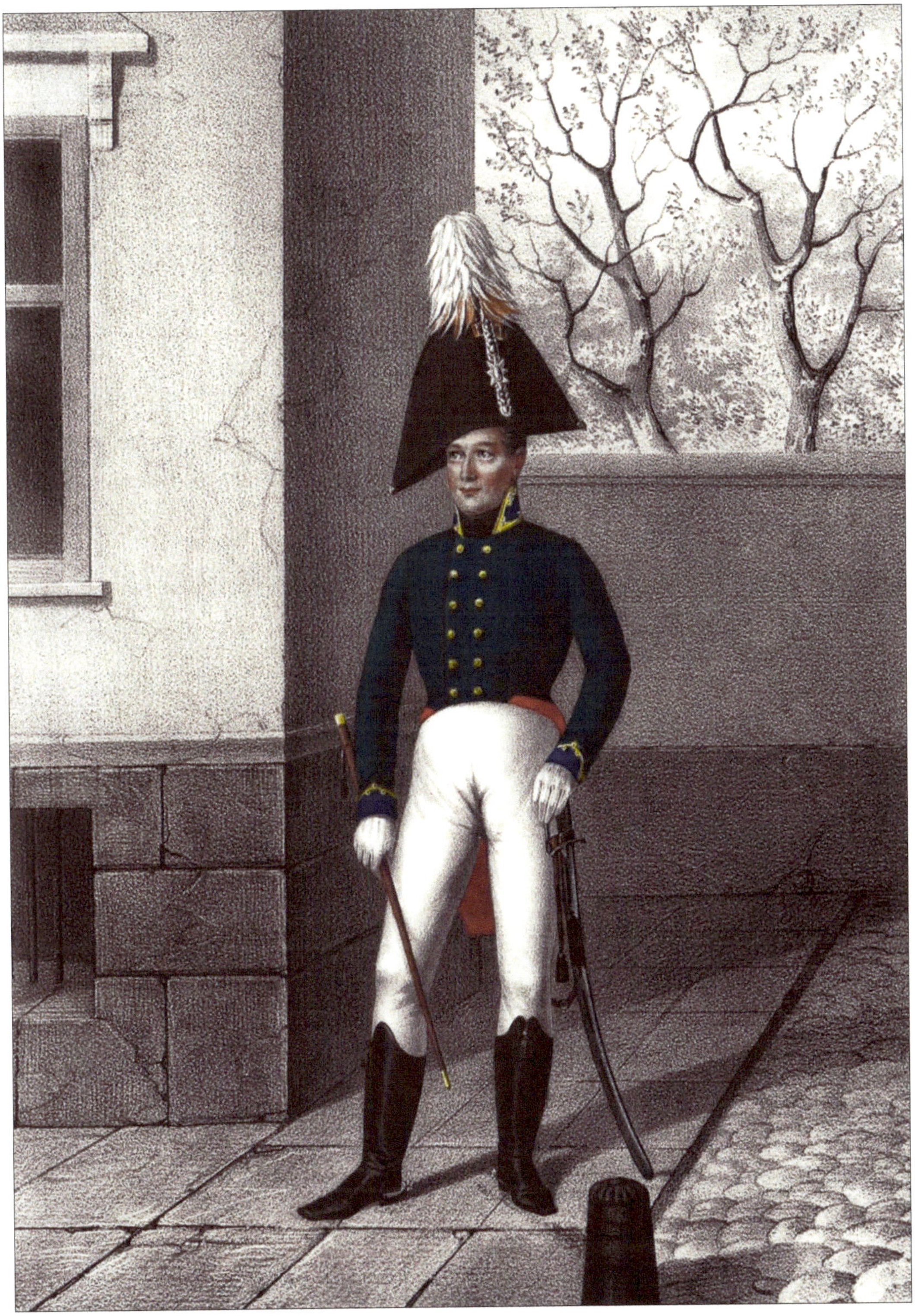

Officer. Izyum Hussar Regiment. 1802-1803.

Private and Trumpeter. Belorussia Hussar Regiment 1803-1809.

Noncommissioned Officer's Shako. Belorussia Hussar Regiment. 1803-1809.

Officer and Staff-Trumpeter. Odessa Hussar Regiment. 1803.

Trumpeter. Aleksandriya Hussar Regiment. 1803-1809.

Officer and Trumpeter. Grodno Hussar Regiment. 1806-1809.

Private. Lubny Hussar Regiment. 1807-1809.

Company-grade Officer. Lubny Hussar Regiment. 1808-1810.

Private. Mariupol Hussar Regiment. 1809-1811.

Privates. Pavlograd, Aleksandriya, and Sumy Hussar Regiments. 1809-1811.

Noncommissioned Officers. Akhtyrka and Yelisavetgrad Hussar Regiments. 1808-1811.

Trumpeter. Olviopol Hussar Regiment. 1809-1811.

Staff-Trumpeters. Izyum and Belorussia Hussar Regiments. 1809-1811.

Officers. Grodno and Izyum Hussar Regiments. 1809-1811.

Officer and Privates. Grodno Hussar Regiment. 1812-1817.

FOfficer and Noncommissioned Officer. Irkutsk Hussar Regiment. 1813-1817.

Hussar shako (with badge for distinction). 1814.

Field and Company-grade Officers. Olviopol Hussar Regiment. 1814.

Company-grade Officer and NCO. Aleksandriya Hussar Regiment. 1814-1819.

Rifle. 1814-1825.

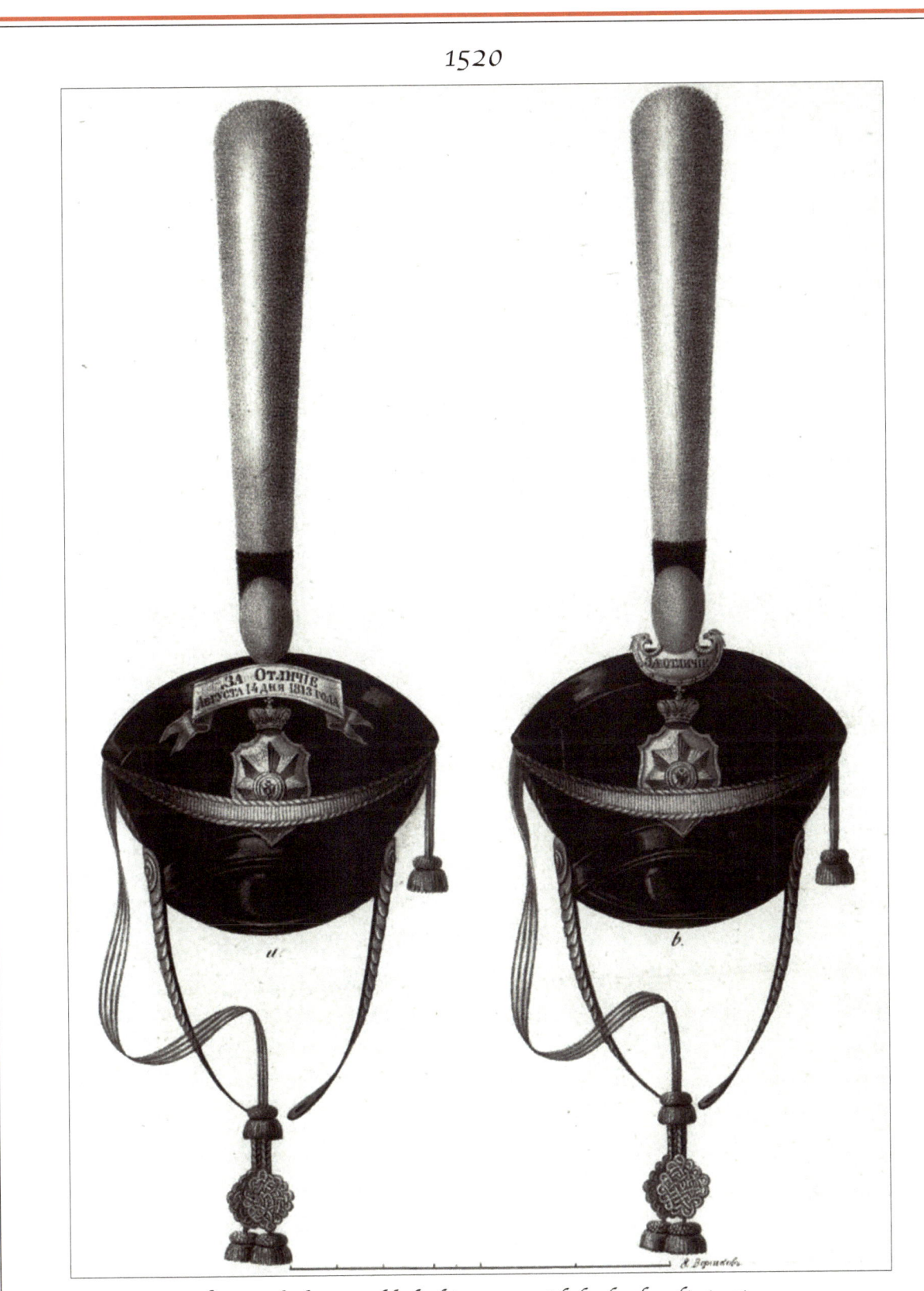

Hussar shakos, established in 1817, with badge for distinction.

Trumpeter. Grodno Hussar Regiment. 1817-1819.

Officer and Private. Izyum Hussar Regiment. 1817-1819.

Privates. Sumy and Grodno Hussar Regiments. 1820.

Noncommissioned Officers. Grodno, Lubny, and Izyum Hussar Regiments. 1820.

Trumpeters. Pavlograd and Yelisavetgrad Hussar Regiments. 1820.

1526

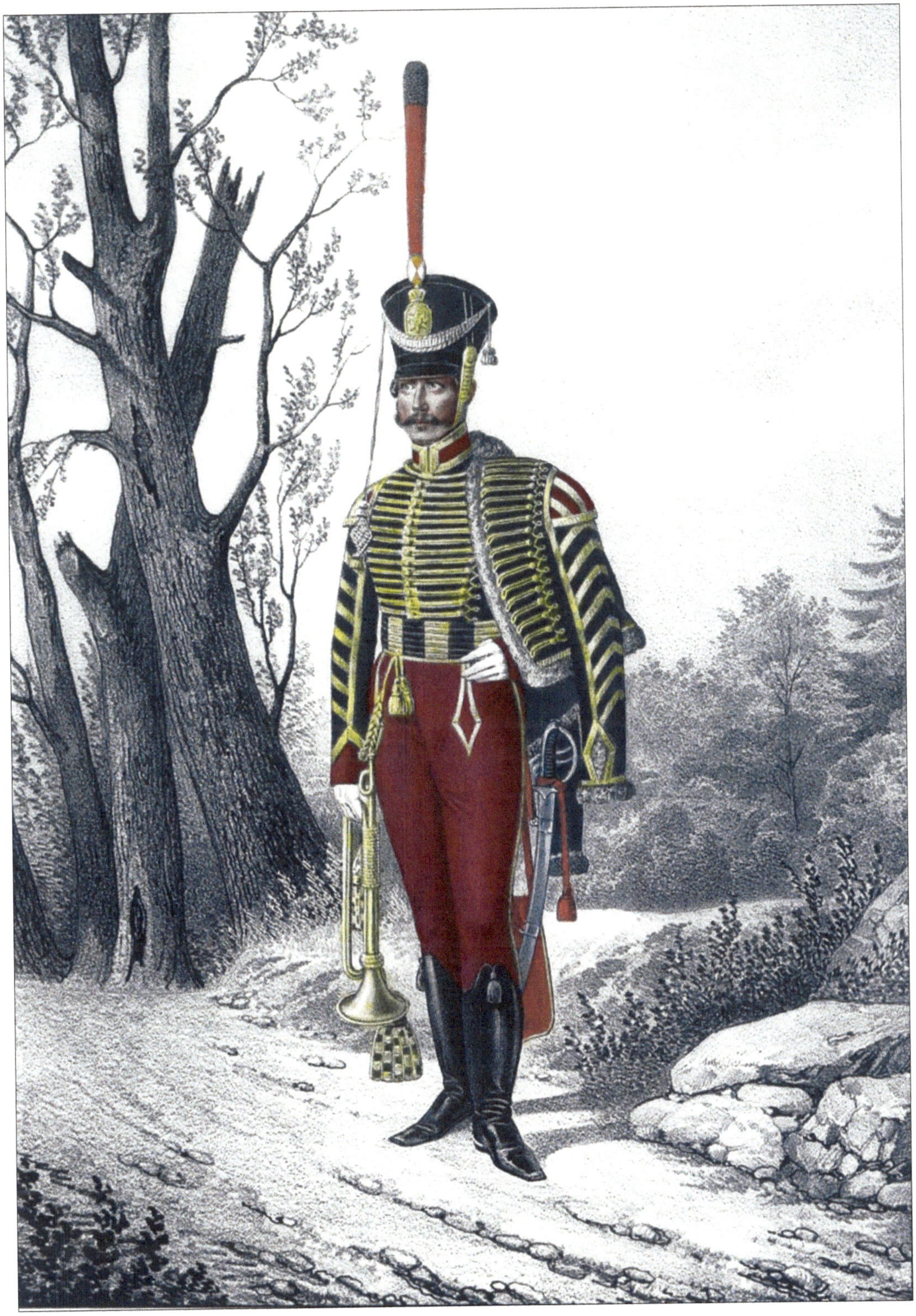

Staff-Trumpeter. Irkutsk Hussar Regiment. 1820.

Officers. Akhtyrka and Aleksandriya Hussar Regiments. 1820.

Field-grade Officers. Mariupol and The Prince of Orange's Hussar Regiments. 1820.

Company-grade Officers. The Prince of Orange's Hussar Regiment. 1820-1825.

Comrade and Ranker. Tatar-Lithuanian Regiment. 1801-1803.

Officer. Tatar-Lithuanian Regiment. 1801-1803.

Officer and Comrade. Polish Horse Regiment. 1801-1803.

Shapka Headdresses. 1803-1808.

Comrades. Tatar and Lithuanian Horse Regiments. 1803-1806.

Privates. his highness the Tsesarevich Constantine Pavlovich's Lancer Regiment. 1803-1806.

NCO. his highness the Tsesarevich Constantine Pavlovich's Lancer Regiment. 1803-1806.

Trumpeters, his highness the Tsesarevich Constantine Pavlovich's Lancer Regiment. 1803-1806.

Officer. his highness the Tsesarevich Constantine Pavlovich's Lancer Regiment. 1803-1806.

Noncommissioned Officer. Polish Horse Regiment. 1805-1806.

Privates. his highness the Tsesarevich Constantine Pavlovich's Lancer Regiment. 1806-1808.

NCO. his highness the Tsesarevich Constantine Pavlovich's Lancer Regiment. 1808 and 1809.

Noncommissioned Officer. Polish Horse Regiment. 1808-1811.

Trumpeter. Tatar Lancer Regiment. 1808-1811.

Staff-Trumpeter. Lithuania Lancer Regiment. 1808-1811.

Private and Field-grade Officer. Volhynia Lancer Regiment. 1808-1811.

Officer's and Soldier's Shapka Headdresses. Tatar Lancer Regiment. 1808-1811.

Privates. Chuguev Lancer Regiment. 1808-1811.

Officer of the Yamburg Lancer Regiment. NCO of the Orenburg Lancer Regiment. 1812-1814.

Trumpeter. Izyum Lancer Regiment. 1812-1814.

Private and Staff-Trumpeter. Siberia Lancer Regiment. 1812-1814.

Company-grade Officer. Vladimir Lancer Regiment. 1812-1814.

Field-grade Officer and Private. Taganrog Lancer Regiment. 1812-1814.

Private. Serpukhov Lancer Regiment. 1812-1814.

Company-grade Officer and Private. Serpukhov Lancer Regiment. 1814-1818.

Company-grade Officers. Serpukhov Lancer Regiment. 1815-1818.

Private. 1st Bug Lancer Regiment. 1817 and 1818.

Private and Noncommissioned Officer. 2nd Bug Lancer Regiment. 1817 and 1818.

Trumpeter. 3rd Bug Lancer Regiment. 1817 and 1818.

Private and Company-grade Officer. 4th Bug Lancer Regiment. 1817 and 1818.

Private. Polish Lancer Regiment. 1818 and 1819.

Noncommissioned Officer. Tatar Lancer Regiment. 1818 and 1819.

Trumpeter. Lithuania Lancer Regiment. 1818 and 1819.

Field-grade Officer. Volhynia Lancer Regiment. 1818 and 1819.

Soldier's and Officer's Shapka Headdresses. Volhynia Lancer Regiment. 1818 and 1819.

Private and Officer. 1st Ukraine Lancer Regiment. 1818 and 1819.

Noncommissioned Officer. 2nd Ukraine Lancer Regiment. 1818 and 1819.

Trumpeter and Private. 3rd Ukraine Lancer Regiment. 1818 and 1819.

Field-grade Officer. 4th Ukraine Lancer Regiment. 1818 and 1819.

Noncommissioned Officer. 4th Ukraine Lancer Regiment. 1819.

Field-grade Officer and Private. Vladimir Lancer Regiment. 1819-1825.

Noncommissioned Officer. Siberia Lancer Regiment. 1819-1825.

1572

Trumpeter. Orenburg Lancer Regiment. 1819-1820.

Company-grade Officer. Yamburg Lancer Regiment. 1819-1825.

Privates. Taganrog and Chuguev Lancer Regiments. 1819-1825.

Staff-Trumpeters. Borisoglebsk and Taganrog Lancer Regiments. 1819-1825.

Private. 1st Ukraine Lancer Regiment. 1819-1825.

Noncommissioned Officers. 2nd, 3rd, and 4th Ukraine Lancer Regiments. 1819-1825.

Noncommissioned Officers. 1st and 2nd Bug Lancer Regiments. 1819-1825.

Company-grade Officers. 3rd and 4th Bug Lancer Regiments. 1819-1825.

Privates. Polish Lancer Regiment. 1819-1825.

Noncommissioned Officer. Tatar Lancer Regiment. 1819-1825.

Trumpeter. Lithuania Lancer Regiment. 1819-1825.

Field-grade Officer and Company-grade Officer. Volhynia Lancer Regiment. 1819-1825.

Trumpeters. Volhynia Lancer Regiment. 1820-1825.

Privates. Gendarme Regiment. 1815-1817.

Noncommissioned Officer. Gendarme Regiment. 1815-1817.

Trumpeter and Staff-Trumpeter. Gendarme Regiment. 1815-1817.

Company-grade Officer. Gendarme Regiment. 1815-1817.

Field-grade Officers. Gendarme Regiment. 1815-1817.

Field-grade Officers. Gendarme Regiment. 1815-1825.

Noncommissioned Officer and Company-grade Officer. Gendarme Regiment. 1817-1825.

Private. Gendarme Regiment. 1817-1820.

Noncommissioned Officer and Trumpeter. Gendarme Regiment. 1820-1825.

Privates. Train Battalions. 1819 and 1820.

Noncommissioned Officers. Train Battalions. 1819 and 1820.

Company-grade Officers. Train Battalions. 1819 and 1820.

Noncommissioned Officer and Company-grade Officer. Train Battalions. 1820-1825.

Noncommissioned Officer. Lithuania Train Brigade. 1820-1825.

Company-grade Officer. Train Battalions of the Grenadier Corps. 1821-1825.

Company-grade Officer. Lithuania Train Brigade. 1822-1825.

Noncommissioned Officer. 1st Battalion of the Lithuania Train Brigade. 1823-1825.

Private and Company-grade Officer. 1st Battalion of the Lithuania Train Brigade. 1823-1825.

SOLDIERS, WEAPONS & UNIFORMS ALREADY PUBLISHED
(TITLES ALREADY PUBLISHED)

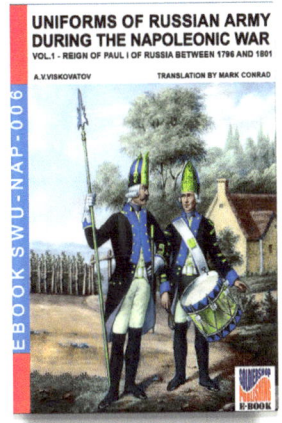

UNIFORMS OF RUSSIAN ARMY DURING THE NAPOLEONIC WAR
VOL.1 - REIGN OF PAUL I OF RUSSIA BETWEEN 1796 AND 1801
A.V.VISKOVATOV — TRANSLATION BY MARK CONRAD
EBOOK SWU-NAP-006

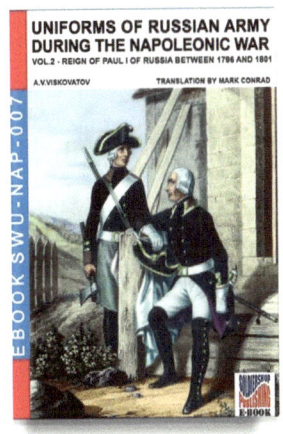

UNIFORMS OF RUSSIAN ARMY DURING THE NAPOLEONIC WAR
VOL.2 - REIGN OF PAUL I OF RUSSIA BETWEEN 1796 AND 1801
A.V.VISKOVATOV — TRANSLATION BY MARK CONRAD
EBOOK SWU-NAP-007

UNIFORMS OF RUSSIAN ARMY DURING THE NAPOLEONIC WAR
VOL.3 - REIGN OF PAUL I 1796 AND 1801 - THE CAVALRY
A.V.VISKOVATOV — TRANSLATION BY MARK CONRAD
EBOOK SWU-NAP-008

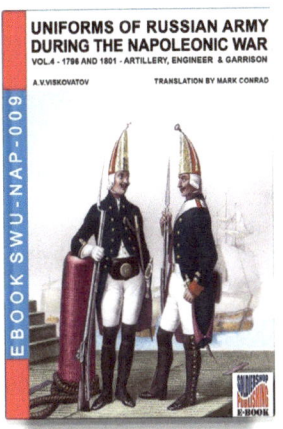

UNIFORMS OF RUSSIAN ARMY DURING THE NAPOLEONIC WAR
VOL.4 - 1796 AND 1801 - ARTILLERY, ENGINEER & GARRISON
A.V.VISKOVATOV — TRANSLATION BY MARK CONRAD
EBOOK SWU-NAP-009

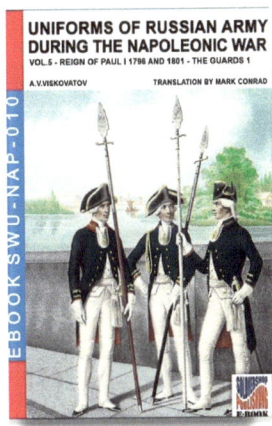

UNIFORMS OF RUSSIAN ARMY DURING THE NAPOLEONIC WAR
VOL.5 - REIGN OF PAUL I 1796 AND 1801 - THE GUARDS 1
A.V.VISKOVATOV — TRANSLATION BY MARK CONRAD
EBOOK SWU-NAP-010

UNIFORMS OF RUSSIAN ARMY DURING THE NAPOLEONIC WAR
VOL.6 - REIGN OF PAUL I 1796 AND 1801 - THE GUARDS 2
A.V.VISKOVATOV — TRANSLATION BY MARK CONRAD
EBOOK SWU-NAP-011

UNIFORMS OF RUSSIAN ARMY DURING THE NAPOLEONIC WAR
VOL.7 - REIGN OF PAUL I 1796 AND 1801 - FLAGS & STANDARDS
A.V.VISKOVATOV — TRANSLATION BY MARK CONRAD
EBOOK SWU-NAP-012

UNIFORMS OF RUSSIAN ARMY DURING THE NAPOLEONIC WAR
VOL.8 - REIGN OF ALEXANDER I 1801-1825 THE GRENADIERS
A.V.VISKOVATOV — TRANSLATION BY MARK CONRAD
EBOOK SWU-NAP-013

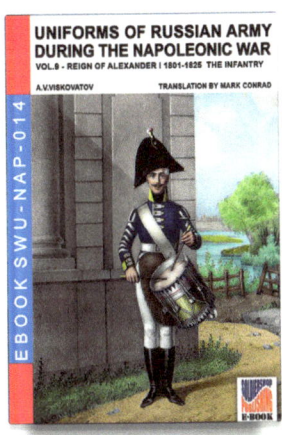

UNIFORMS OF RUSSIAN ARMY DURING THE NAPOLEONIC WAR
VOL.9 - REIGN OF ALEXANDER I 1801-1825 THE INFANTRY
A.V.VISKOVATOV — TRANSLATION BY MARK CONRAD
EBOOK SWU-NAP-014

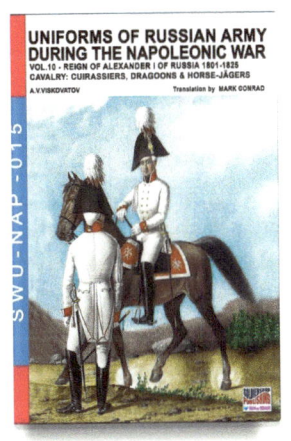

UNIFORMS OF RUSSIAN ARMY DURING THE NAPOLEONIC WAR
VOL.10 - REIGN OF ALEXANDER I OF RUSSIA 1801-1825
CAVALRY: CUIRASSIERS, DRAGOONS & HORSE-JÄGERS
A.V.VISKOVATOV — Translation by MARK CONRAD
SWU-NAP-015

UNIFORMS OF RUSSIAN ARMY DURING THE NAPOLEONIC WAR
VOL.11 - REIGN OF ALEXANDER I OF RUSSIA 1801-1825
CAVALRY: HUSSARS, LANCERS, GENDARMES, & THE TRAIN
A.V.VISKOVATOV — Translation by MARK CONRAD
SWU-NAP-016

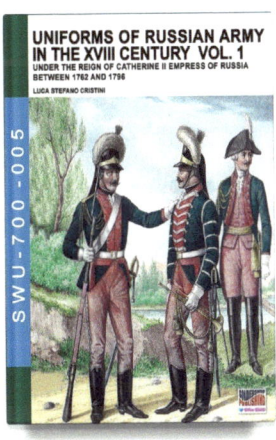

UNIFORMS OF RUSSIAN ARMY IN THE XVIII CENTURY VOL. 1
UNDER THE REIGN OF CATHERINE II EMPRESS OF RUSSIA
BETWEEN 1762 AND 1796
LUCA STEFANO CRISTINI
SWU-700-005